THE BRITISH
Their Identity and Their Religion

DANIEL JENKINS

THE BRITISH
THEIR IDENTITY
AND THEIR
RELIGION

SCM PRESS LTD

334 00131 5

First published 1975
by SCM Press Ltd
58 Bloomsbury Street WC1

© SCM Press Ltd 1975

Type set by Gloucester Typesetting Co.

Printed and bound in Great Britain by
Redwood Burn Limited
Trowbridge & Esher

Contents

Why this book came to be written

There is evidence that all is not well with communal life in modern Britain. This means that a fresh look must be taken at ourselves and our institutions, but it is one of the symptoms of our sickness that most of us are extremely reluctant to take it. We are not sure any more who we are, and, therefore, our relationship to what helped our predecessors to reach self-definition is embarrassed and reluctant. This partly accounts for the feverish hedonism and the related obsession with economic matters which are a feature of the public scene. We can think of nothing better to do with ourselves.

This book is an attempt to take a fresh look at two aspects of British life which are relatively neglected today, those concerned with nationality and religion. While the choice of these reflects my own commitments and interests, anyone who considers the people of Britain in the light of their history, including quite recent history, can hardly deny their importance. What may give a measure of originality to this attempt is my conviction that these two aspects are much more closely related than it has been customary to suppose. This enquiry began by looking at churches as institutions in the context of the wider life of the community, but as it developed, it became clear that for most British people, questions of church allegiance, and of the attitudes and styles of living associated with church allegiance, are intimately linked in their minds with wider communal loyalties.

This becomes particularly manifest the more those wider loyalties are narrowed down to the separate national groups who make up the United Kingdom. The more I considered what it means in specific terms to be distinctively English, Scottish or Welsh, the more important became the place of religious inheritance in the process of definition. And the further away I moved from looking at the churches as a professional theologian, and the more I tried to examine them as a social historian might, the more obvious it became. It has been particularly true within the history of the separate nations who make up Britain that the churches have 'preserved society, kept it together, strengthened it', and that by its religious rites 'the social group reaffirms itself periodically'.[1]

The importance of this fact is only partially diminished if we happen to believe that churches and the national consciousness with which they are involved are both in irreversible decline. As we shall see, there are plenty of reasons for suggesting caution before accepting this irreversibility. The movement of religious attitudes is notoriously incalculable and a resurgence of national conscious- ness has already taken place against all the odds in Scotland and Wales, a resurgence which is beginning to have its repercussions in parts of England also. But even if our churches and separate nations are dying, their situation would still merit serious atten- tion. The business of providing for their old age, arranging a decent termination and interment, clearing up after them and disposing of their substantial estates, which include many of our most precious and best-kept communal possessions, and filling up the places they have left vacant, all adds up to a formidable under- taking. If, however, they are not dying but passing through a difficult and uncertain period of change, their situation continues to require serious study and discussion.

This becomes the more true if, as some of the evidence implies, a large number of the other traditional British institutions are facing similar difficulties. If churches languish, so do many voluntary charitable organizations and, at the local level at least, so does active membership in political parties. The armed services, the judiciary, the police, the medical profession and now the universities, do not hold the same places in public esteem that they did until quite recently.[2] This suggests that the causes of our much-canvassed religious decline are related to a wider communal malaise and are likely to be as much cultural as directly religious. The one cannot be adequately considered without reference to the other.

The other reasons why this book came to be written are much more internal to the life of the Christian community. As a theologian, I have come to see with increasing clarity that the theologian's task cannot be undertaken without explicit reference to the social context in which the Christian community finds itself at a particular time. This is not to imply for a moment that that context must necessarily determine the way in which the theologian works, only that it is one factor which cannot be ignored. Where I might differ from some of those who accept the title of 'political' theologians is in defining what that social context is. It is necessary to strive to see one's own situation in as wide a setting as possible, but it is no less necessary to start from where one is. Where we start from in Britain is the British situation and that situation as seen from the perspective of the British churches. That may be regrettably undramatic, but it is a fact.

Apart from anything else, if we fail to take this into account, a great deal of what theologians, and church leaders, say about the ecumenical movement arouses little interest outside very narrowly defined church circles. Relations between churches are affected just as much by national and regional loyalties and inherited cultural styles and class interests as they are by matters of doctrine or ritual or organization. It is true, and important, that a fresh religious experience can quickly break through these and put them back in their properly subordinate place, but in its absence these factors loom large, and even when it is present they still affect the situation. Thus, efforts by professional clerics to unite divided churches revolve largely around discussions of the doctrine of the ministry and, to a lesser extent, of the sacraments. Real issues are involved in these discussions, but it requires elaborate training in the imaginative appropriation of a great deal of past experience to see what they are. For most people, they only come alive when they are related to such matters as those of establishment by the state, of 'no bishop, no king', or of ancestral fears among the Scots and Welsh of English attempts to impose their own system upon them. Most British people are not likely to recover living Christian faith or to participate with any enthusiasm in any new ecclesiastical alignment except through a fresh understanding of their heritage, which they incline to think of primarily in distinctively English, Scottish or Welsh terms.

A third reason for looking at these questions in a Christian context is even more down-to-earth. They are frequently looked at in an un-Christian way, and not least by professional Christian spokesmen themselves. Most English people identify being British with being English and find it hard to treat distinctive Scottish or Welsh nationality as anything but an amusing or tiresome eccentricity. Scots and Welsh people bitterly resent this, and in a time when all national and regional groups, but especially smaller ones, feel threatened by the centralizing and standardizing influence of modern economic and social organization, they find it easy to put the blame for their ills on the apparently arrogant English. This, in its turn, irritates the English, who are tempted to write off the Scots and the Welsh as touchy and cantankerous victims of an inferiority complex. Church loyalty and national loyalty are so closely linked, especially in Scotland and Wales, and the sense of the past is so strong in church life, that this becomes even more visible in church relationships than elsewhere.

This is a situation which no responsible Christian can accept. Christian leaders should be able to foresee possible occasions of conflict, especially within the Christian community itself, and then quietly take steps to help to resolve situations and create possibilities of reconciliation before communication breaks down. They are meant to be *pontifices*, bridge-builders. With the consequences of the scandalous failure of those who bear a Christian name to do this before our eyes in Northern Ireland, it is hardly necessary to remind ourselves of its importance in the rest of what is meant to be the United Kingdom. The English cannot bring themselves to believe that something like a 'colonialist' situation exists within Great Britain, and consequently some Scots and Welsh self-righteously consider themselves excused from having to think in a Christian way about their English relatives and neighbours. Yet in a time when we not only need each other but also the best of each other, which is often the most distinctive, insensitivity on the one hand and resentment on the other will succeed only in bringing out the worst in all of us who make up the British people. Were this to happen, professional churchmen will have to accept a more than average share of the blame. But there is no reason at all why it should happen. In its effort to speak plainly about our differences and to restate what we have in common, as churches and as nations, I hope that this book can make some contribution to the restoration of the Christian unity of the people of Britain.

NOTES

1. A description of Durkheim's views using these words is given in Joan Brothers, *Religious Institutions*, Longman 1971, p. 8, which could well have been written with Britain in mind.

2. For what such evidence is worth, this was the finding of a survey conducted for *The Times* by the Opinion Research Centre and published in *The Times* under the heading 'Public losing confidence in most of the leading British institutions', on 30 April 1974.

I

THE MATTER OF BRITAIN

I *Is there a matter of Britain ?*

In his book on the architecture of London, that engagingly enthusiastic critic, Ian Nairn, praises the greatness of Wren's St Paul's:

> Here once and for all the principle of English freedom has been given spiritual form; license and variety in the parts, conforming not by order but from free will . . . Compromise was his by nature, and in a sense far deeper than our present recourse to lowest common denominators. So each bay is both Gothic and classical, vigorously discrete and subordinate at the same time to the whole mass . . . The dome is an utter repose which transcends passion instead of ignoring it . . . It is a stupendous, encompassing achievement of balanced feeling and maturity and one that has come to the top again and again in this funny-shaped island just off Europe; Shakespeare's last plays but also what England seems to have called out of people like Handel and T. S. Eliot. It is hard not to sound like a bad Churchillian parody, but in fact this is why we fought the war.[1]

As he shamefacedly recognizes, the style goes astray towards the end of that passage, but what he is saying is true and expresses what many English people would believe to the core of their being. That, however, is not why it is quoted. For what is revealing is that, despite his Scottish name and despite his exceptionally sympathetic understanding of many Scottish and Welsh places, Mr Nairn here appears to overlook that the Welsh and the Scots, not to say many other people, also fought the war on the same side. Did all these others fight only for England, even the England of Wren and

Shakespeare and of Handel's and T. S. Eliot's adoption? It was certainly part of what they fought for, because that England has a claim on all who value the greatest expressions of the human spirit and a special claim on those who share the British heritage with the English. But are the rest of us altogether out of order in feeling a tinge of resentment when we contemplate the grandeur of Wren's St Paul's, and want only to be united with English people in admiration and gratitude, at being told that this was the expression of something uniquely English and that the war was fought to preserve it?

Now we can be confident that, if he were challenged, Mr Nairn would want to reply that he did not mean to be taken in this sense. After all, he does speak of 'this funny-shaped island off the continent' and would probably agree that the Scottish and the Welsh strains contribute to the quality which he so much admires. Yet it is worth taking him up on the point because the fact that even someone so knowledgeable and sympathetic as Mr Nairn slips as a matter of course into speaking of this as English, and distinctively English, not only reveals where the trouble lies between the English, the Scots and the Welsh, but also shows a misunderstanding of where much of the strength of the admirable quality itself is to be found. The independence with a strong public sense and 'the repose which transcends passion without ignoring it', are surely universal qualities of human maturity. All the greatest art expresses them in some measure and they evoke a response, as St Paul's was meant to, which speaks not of that which is distinctive of one sectional heritage but of that which binds us together as members of the human family before God. We can agree that the greatest figures of the Elizabethan period and the seventeenth century, of which St Paul's might be taken as the architectural apotheosis, expressed these qualities more nobly and more eloquently than any others have done in our national life. What is questionable is whether it was the distinctively and definably English strain alone which did this.

After all, this was the period in which the great division in British life emerged clearly into the open. St Paul's does express balance in tension, but the balance was not simply that achieved by the party which finally triumphed in the ecclesiastical debates of the seventeenth century. It would lack its universal quality if it were only a celebration of the spirit of 1688, still less of 1662. It was a representation of the best of what was in these, but it also pointed beyond them and, in so far as it holds a tension, the other parties to the debate were on one side of it. It is the London of Milton, the Milton both of the prose pamphlets and of the epics, as well as the London of Andrewes which finds balance and fulfilment in St Paul's. Nor, even in the seventeenth century, were the Scottish and Welsh strains absent. For what it was worth, the Tudors were Welsh, and there was a good deal of the Welsh, for good or ill, in Henry VIII and Elizabeth. The Stuarts, again for good or for ill, were Scots. As a reminder of how complicated these things are, Cromwell, the Huntingdonshire squire who preferred even the Cavaliers to the Scots, could be taken as the representative of the English balancing factor against a Scottish king married to a French wife, a king who conspicuously did not understand balance in tension, a failure which cost him his head.[2]

In fact this quality of balance in tension in British life has not been particularly characteristic of the life of the 'Establishment' English ever since St Paul's was completed. St Paul's was a memorial to the spirit of the seventeenth century rather than an expression of what came to the fore in English life in the eighteenth. The public life of England between the Restoration and the Reform Bill showed little of the spirit Ian Nairn found in St Paul's. It was not until Gladstone, who was the first outstanding political leader since Cromwell to understand balance in tension,[3] stepped over to become the leader of those whose vision of society was significantly different from that of the ascendancy, and Disraeli was stimulated to reformulate conservative ideals, that there was any creative tension to balance. Politics was largely a matter of keeping power in the hands of the landed interest with the minimum of upheaval and of ignoring or even suppressing the rest, unless, like the Edinburgh Scots and the London Dissenters, they proved themselves well-behaved or, like the leaders of the Industrial Revolution, they became so powerful as to need mollifying and conversion to Establishment ways.

Thus it is not inconceivable, given generosity of vision on the part of those who regained power and a more mellow temper on the part of those who were cast out, that the Church of England might have tried to rebuild the broken fragments of British unity after the Reformation and have become a truly national church, a *via media* which kept herself open to influence both from the left and from the right. It did not happen, and what emerged was the age of English empiricism or, as its critics would prefer to describe it, of shrunken imagination, in which men refused to see further than their noses lest they might find something new and disturbing. For the most part, the Church of England gave up trying to be representative of the nation as a whole and contented itself with being the spiritual arm of the propertied classes. When it did 'get religion in its old age', in the late eighteenth and the nineteenth centuries, it did so mainly in 'denominational' rather than truly national form, whether the denominations happened to call themselves 'evangelical' or 'catholic'. Romanticism and the religious and political revivals of the late eighteenth and early nineteenth centuries did reintroduce creative tension to British life, but it was only fitfully, in the experience of outstanding individuals, that any balance was achieved. For the most part, the differing parties were more conscious of their separation from each other than of their unity.

In fact, it has only been in the twentieth century that something like genuine social unity has emerged in British as a whole. In retrospect, the years from 1940 to 1960 may look like almost the only period in our history when the British have been a substantially united people, far more so than in the Victorian heyday of imperial glory. The increasing internationalization of life, the partial redistribution of wealth, adult suffrage, the extension of educational opportunity and the rise of the ecumenical movement have all been factors in producing this situation. It is a pity that we lacked the imagination to see and make the most of all the opportunities for new development which that period gave, because present circumstances are much less favourable. Social and economic groups have become more divided from each other, our population has become more mixed and transient without becoming more integrated, and the 'public sense' which strengthens loyalty to institutions has markedly diminished.

This means that those who recognize the importance of the separate strands in the British tradition and are still convinced of their value have a new kind of responsibility to each other. They will acknowledge that they have more in common than either has with those who have no such recognition, yet they will avoid making this an excuse for advocating the kind of coalition which is no more than a way of persuading your opponents to accept your policies without loss of face. Experience over the last couple of generations should have made them see clearly that they not only need each other but also the best of each other, and that the best is often the most distinctive. We cannot ignore what has divided us in the past, and it would be wrong to try to do so, but it is possible so to interpret those divisions as to enrich and not to diminish new-found unity in the present.

Nairn saw that in St Paul's and contrasted it with what he called our modern search for the lowest common denominator. That may be unfair, but it is true that what used to be called 'Butskellism', the safe and sensible mediocrity of the centre, has been the dominant feature of British life, in church and general cultural life as well as in politics, for many years. It is this which may have been one factor in producing the curiously irritable and ineffectual reaction of the sixties. Young people did not seem to know what they wanted, except that it was not their own past as presented to them in the bland, predictable and unexciting persons of their immediate predecessors. This is a reason why it is not enough simply to strengthen the consensus in modern society, necessary though that may be in industrial and economic life. We shall not discover anything new for the future unless we dig deeper into the past than most of us are disposed to do and draw strength from what our forefathers at their best saw, in their unity and their division, and then appropriate that best from our related but separate traditions as we try to see what should be done now. In this context, the revival of national consciousness in Scotland and Wales could be interpreted as a positively hopeful sign, always provided that it becomes the preface to a better international conversation rather than a resentful retreat to the hills. This is why it is so vital for the English to see that to be British is something different from being English in different sorts of ways and that the British ideal is one which incorporates and does not ignore what is distinctive in being Scottish and being Welsh.

Even when all allowance is made for English dominance, and for the healthy British readiness to leave well alone, it is curious that so little attention has been given in the past to the matter of British, as distinct from purely English, identity. After the First World War, there was a strong wave of self-consciousness about national identity and about differences between nations, partly because it was seen to be bound up with the principle of national self-determination and with the League of Nations. Salvador de Madariaga wrote his book on the English, Spanish and French characters and Ernest Barker wrote his large book on *National Character*.[4] Americans have always been fascinated by England and Emerson's *Traits of the English* and Santayana's essays, *Soliloquies in England*,[5] are still worth reading. But, although Barker has some pertinent things to say of the Scots, the focus has always been on England. Sociologists, in their very fashion-dominated subject, have always been more ready to study matters of class or status than of nationality, yet it is not self-evident that these are any less impalpable than a sense of national identity. The Registrar-General's well-known classification by occupation has been heavily relied on to give the semblance of objectivity to their judgments on these matters, while the study of nationality has been left to the historians or novelists. Yet even among these it has been generally the English, the Scots or the Welsh who have been separately dealt with, except where British has been used as a synonym for English. Even someone so exceptionally well-informed as Sir Denis Brogan in his book on *The English People*,[6] said nothing about the British ideal, although he was, of course, well aware that the Scots and the Welsh are different, with their own distinctive links with America. Mr George Orwell, in his interesting contribution on the working-classes to the curiously entitled 'Britain in Pictures' series, presented a useful corrective to some of the other pictures of England given in that series but also assumed the monolithically English nature of working-class life, which was not true even of those working-class people residing in England.[7] Mr A. L. Morton published in 1966 a book of essays with the title *The Matter of Britain*, but although it began with a discussion of the Arthurian cycle, his romantic Communism did not prevent him from considering British culture in exclusively English terms.[8] Dr A. L. Rowse, in his essay on *The English Spirit*,[9] is emphatic that he, a Cornishman, is not English, but he does not specify what binds Cornishmen, as well as other Celts, to the English in the common British identity which he would readily acknowledge. Dr Kitson Clark's *The English Inheritance: A Historical Essay*[10] is the book whose approach is nearest to what we have in mind, although from a conservative and Anglican rather than a radical and Free Church perspective, but it is significant that he firmly excludes Scotland and Wales from his consideration.

Modern American scholars are remarkably thorough students of British affairs, who often disconcert us by knowing more about us than we do ourselves, but so far none of them has produced any significant work on the modern matter of Britain. Most of them are fascinated by distinctively English literature and history. Those who are interested in Scotland and Wales are either concerned with the links between their ancestors from those countries and America or with Celtic studies. Among the British themselves, most of the interest shown in Britain as distinct from English history is in the remote past. It is archaeological, or related to Roman or Arthurian studies, or it is the work of the poetic imagination. Geoffrey Ashe, *Camelot and the Vision of Albion*,[11] tries to relate the Arthurian legend to modern ideals for Britain, but in very generalized terms. Charles Williams' poetic sequences, *Taliessin through Logres* and *The Region of the Summer Stars*, deal with the matter of Britain and its Christian roots, but it requires a considerable imaginative effort to see any direct significance for the present day in them.[12] This is even more true of David Jones' *Anathemata*, despite his description of it as the work of 'a Londoner, of Welsh and English parentage, of Protestant upbringing, of Catholic subscription', which draws heavily upon Welsh and

Latin language and experience 'within a kind of Cockney setting'.[13]

The ideal of Britishness is not, however, as recondite as all this suggests. The real reason why it has not been examined more closely, or defined more precisely, has been that it has worked and that, until very recently, people have been content with the way in which it has worked. Self-consciousness about it now becomes necessary because it is no longer working well enough. The Scots and the Welsh are protesting against being pushed to the margin of life in Britain, and the new demands made upon our sense of national identity by joining the European Economic Community have to be met. The recently published *Royal Commission on the Constitution, 1969–1973*[14] is a belated recognition that this is a matter which must now receive public attention. It has the merit also of recognizing clearly that there is a definite British identity, that 'the United Kingdom has been greater than the sum of its constituent parts',[15] while at the same time trying to do justice to the distinctive elements in those separate nations which make up those parts. What it does not do, perhaps inevitably in such a document, is to analyse what these distinctive elements are. This may be one reason, among the more obvious ones, for the cool reception which the majority report has received outside Scotland and Wales, even in Parliament itself. English people, especially metropolitan English people, have not been made to see how much their own understanding of themselves is affected by Scottish and Welsh elements in our community life.

However difficult this analysis may be, an attempt to make it can no longer be avoided. There is a danger of each of the separate nations turning in upon themselves under the pressure of existence in a world changing rapidly in ways which are not to their advantage. In the process, we may lose our British identity and gain only a querulous and backward-looking Englishness, Scottishness or Welshness, which emphasize the worst and not the best qualities of each people. It is only those who are sure of their identity who have the courage to be outgoing, and it is only those who have the courage to be outgoing who can be assured of their own identity. Englishness, Scottishness and Welshness in themselves have never proved enough to enable people to do this. Britishness has, both within these islands and beyond them, because it holds a larger number of differences in creative tension.

2 *National consciousness and religious heritage*

The connection between national consciousness and religious heritage within the British Isles is very close, yet it also has received curiously little attention. The great strength of the British tradition lies in its ability to give social embodiment to political ideas and to be prepared to modify them in the process. The Germans may be profounder and the French more logical, but the British have a gift for creating the more durable institutions. This may be because the English, the dominant national group, have long cultivated a sense of what is practical and possible. Even their social critics seem to have a greater public impact than most of those on the Continent because, almost instinctively, they have recognized a need to speak specifically and with an awareness of the dynamics of the society of which they are a part. Compare the public influence in their own communities of such nineteenth-century figures as Mill and Ruskin and Arnold and Morris with their European contemporaries like Kant or Dostoevsky or Nietzsche. Or compare the ways in which F. D. Maurice and Kierkegaard set about trying to modify established institutions. Can anyone imagine Kierkegaard starting a Working Men's College or a school for young ladies? Reflective men have held a responsible conviction that it is possible to have some influence on public opinion and even on public policy and have been prepared to direct their efforts to that end. This may be why, at least until very recently, no significant group of vocationally alienated 'intellectuals' on the continental model has grown up in Britain. France is traditionally supposed to be a country where 'intellectuals' have more consideration and public esteem than they obtain elsewhere, but this often seems to be in inverse proportion to their public effectiveness, and many of them take a pride in holding themselves aloof from the great majority of their fellows. In Britain, however, even those who have been most at odds with the established structures of society, like D. H. Lawrence and George Orwell, have retained, in their limited and idiosyncratic way, this strong communal and public sense. The self-discipline and unaffected sense of duty into which almost all parts of the British nation slipped during and for several years after the Second World War, when they were all able to make common cause, revealed how deep and tenacious the roots of this attitude are.

This very fact may explain why so little attention is paid to this matter. Up to now, we have been able to afford to take it, like our common British identity, for granted. But, deep-rooted as this plant may be, it has had to endure the shaking of some violent blasts in recent years, and there is little sign that they are likely to diminish in force. Whereas until recently there were very large numbers of people who could not be sure that they believed in God but were very sure that they believed in England, it now becomes increasingly difficult to invoke the spirit of patriotism without being made to feel either pompous or complacent, unless one is in the fortunate position, as many Scotsmen and Welshmen believe that they are, of being able to harness one's patriotism to resentment against a large-scale concentration of traditional power. The same appears to be happening to a sense of civic pride. The more privileged young people rarely speak with enthusiasm of their home town, and few of them plan to make their careers within it. It sometimes seems that it is only sport which has retained its role as a focus of particularist loyalty held with uncritical fervour.[16] A situation of common danger can, of course, quickly rekindle and concentrate the sense of national identity, but one has not yet arisen in Britain within the conscious memory of even those people who are now approaching middle age. The nearest to such a situation since the Second World War, the Suez crisis of 1956, served to divide the nation as much as it united, in the same way as the much more protracted Vietnam crisis has divided the United States.

To talk of all this as a crisis of national consciousness may be exaggerated, and it is certainly premature. Many commentators at the time spoke of Churchill's funeral, with all its traditional panoply, as the funeral of the old order, but they were speaking the language of Fleet Street, and Fleet Street is not the best place at which to test the depth of the soil from which the common life of Britain draws its real sustenance. All the same, it would be hard to deny that the British are less united as a people than they were twenty years ago and that there is much less implicit agreement among them about a pattern of common life in which the great majority of people could participate in such a way as to evoke a strong loyalty.

This should be a matter of particular concern to the British Christian community. Although it will be one of the major points of this argument that the sense of being Christian is not as consciously related to the sense of being distinctively British as it needs to be, it is undoubtedly closely linked for most Christian people with their sense of being English, Scottish or Welsh. Professor Ernest Barker, in his book *National Character*, described Scotland as being a church rather than a nation. And a quite recent writer has said:

> The roots of Scotland are in the Church of Scotland. The 'Kirk' expresses the character of the Scots more truly and more completely than any other institution.[17]

Not all Scots would agree with this, but it indicates that, in the minds of very large numbers of the most representative and self-conscious Scots people, national consciousness and religious heritage are very closely intertwined. The Welsh tradition, especially since its great revival which started in the eighteenth century, has expressed itself chiefly through distinctively Welsh religious institutions. The Welsh language is most fully itself as a language of religion, and the most popular forms of Welsh song and poetry are hymns. Even the non-religious institutions, like the Eisteddfod, have a strong religious flavour. England is a larger and more diversified country and the relation between religion and the national consciousness is less straightforward and unqualified, but abundant evidence exists to indicate that here also it is very close. The monarchy has an overtly religious character, and much of what is distinctively national in the English heritage is expressed in religious forms. The tower or spire of the parish church is an integral part of the ideal picture of their country which most loyal

Englishmen carry in their minds, and it is to the church that they repair on great national occasions, just as it is in their cathedrals that they place their national memorials. In his book on *The English Spirit*, Dr A. L. Rowse, who is no churchman, found himself constantly writing in the warmest terms about the Church of England. George Herbert seemed to him to represent the ideal of the Englishman just as much as Drake or Nelson.

Quite apart from any formal arrangements made by states and religious establishments, most British people most of the time throughout our modern history have taken it for granted that to be English, Scottish or Welsh is also, in some sense, to be Christian. The Welsh national young people's movement, *Urdd Gobaith Cymru*, claims to stand for Wales, the language and Christ, with the implication that somehow the three are connected. Similarly, it is significant that the Women's Institutes, although emphatic in asserting political and religious neutrality, nevertheless chose Blake's 'Jerusalem' as their song. This is not, of course, to deny that there are many deeply patriotic people who are not religious, nor that there are many others who may subsume their religious loyalty under their patriotic one. It is to say that, both historically and still to a large extent today, the two loyalties are linked. Anything approaching a crisis of national consciousness, therefore, is a matter which should deeply concern those whose primary loyalty is Christian.

The most striking, and topically urgent, example of the close relation between religious heritage and national consciousness in these islands is provided, of course, by Northern Ireland. That this should be so is a source of acute embarrassment to those concerned for the good name of religious institutions because divisions which claim a religious origin and sanction create so much envy, malice and lack of charity. It is, however, a salutary reminder that these issues are by no means dead in the modern world and that, if they are not handled properly, the coalescence of religious, cultural and political divisions still makes the task of reconciliation particularly hard. The Northern Ireland situation is so difficult, has received so much attention and is so germane to the theme of this book that some explanation may seem necessary of why it is not treated in detail. The chief reason, quite apart from the author's lack of qualification for dealing with a matter which is exercising many minds at present, is that it is ultimately much more an Irish than a characteristically British situation. This is so despite the fact that it has repercussions for British life and despite the ostentatious loyalty of the Ulster Unionists to the British Crown. In any case, while Northern Ireland provides us with a warning and plenty of painfully illustrative material, it will not be a main focus of attention in this discussion.

The reference to Northern Ireland may serve, however, to strengthen misgivings that many people are likely to have about the whole of this enquiry. It deals with matters which are of decreasing importance and which can, therefore, be safely left alone. Only the most backward-looking people, living in the most backward places, are likely to be interested. If a crisis is developing in national consciousness, it is only because that consciousness, in common with the religious consciousness which is supposed to be bound up with it, is in decay. There will be many who will want to add, 'And a good thing, too'. Religion and nationalism have caused enough trouble in the world and it is time we moved on to something better, an enlightened supra-national community free from national and religious prejudice. The social factors which have already been described are bound to make them both fade away. Those who believe that there may still be a future for religion (and there is some evidence that, in many contexts, religious loyalties are proving more durable than national ones)[18] will see that its hope lies in dissociating it from national loyalties. Some may want to see the rise of the ecumenical movement in our time as a recognition of this fact. The churches have seen the red light, and it remains an open question as to whether they have seen it in time to save themselves. Modern metropolitan man is a new kind of person. He may or may not be a better or more enlightened person than his predecessors, but he certainly needs a new style of life and patterns of association, and a new focus for his loyalty. The issues being raised here are simply not relevant to his situation, and are likely to become less and less so.

No one can pretend that these matters are at the centre of

popular debate at present, except in places, like parts of Scotland
and Wales, which are remote from the main centres of communication. Nor should it for a moment be denied that metropolitan
living calls for new styles, patterns and foci. Yet it is always
dangerous to extrapolate the future only on the basis of those
trends which are most readily visible at present, and this is a
danger to which metropolitan man, because he lives in the market-
place where people are chiefly interested in a quick sale and rapid
turnover of ideas, is peculiarly exposed. Professor van Peursen of
Leiden illustrates lectures on this theme with slides of drawings of
imaginary cities, machines and vehicles of the future which were
devised in the nineteenth century. It is clear how they all must have
seemed eminently reasonable in the light of the knowledge and
experience available at their time, but events have proved most of
them to be very wide of the mark. In this particular instance, there
are already signs that things are turning out very differently from
what assumptions which have long been taken for granted might
have led us to suppose. This is quite apart from the consideration
already mentioned that if the grip of religion and nationality is
weakening, that very fact raises public issues of great importance.

There is mounting evidence that the roots of religion and
nationality are stronger and more tenacious as well as more
intertwined than most people have believed. By all the rules,
Scottish, and even more Welsh, national consciousness should have
withered almost to the point of disappearance by now, but nothing
of this kind has happened. This is not merely a matter of the rise
and relative strength of nationalistic political parties, although that
is important evidence on the cultural, if not always on the political,
level. It is much more one of the reassertion of a particular conviction of identity, of Scottishness or Welshness, which may or may
not seek political expression but which is deeply felt and often
passionately expressed. Similar reassertions are to be found in
Cornwall and even in some of the more well-defined regions in
England.[19] This is probably part of a world-wide protest against
the impersonality and sameness, the standardized 'packaged'
quality of so much metropolitan life, which becomes more and
more pronounced as the central areas of large cities everywhere are

surrendered to tourists and to the offices of the same international trading companies.

Related to this is the possibility that increasing leisure may turn out to have quite a different effect in many cases from that which is often taken to be inevitable. Leisure makes travel possible and the most obvious things to go to look at are the great monuments of the past. The vast crowds shepherded through cathedrals, galleries, castles and country houses may not have much opportunity for reflection at the time, but what they see must make some impression, and it is a short step to begin thinking about one's own family and its background in history. To do so has an added attraction if it serves to differentiate one from the great mass of one's fellows in the standardized metropolis and forms a link, however tenuous, with a more manageable group of similar background. This kind of awareness of one's history is greatly intensified, of course, by increased educational opportunity and the social confidence which it brings.

In his well known book, *Protestant-Catholic-Jew*,[20] Will Herberg argued that this has been happening for some time in the USA, where the third generation of immigrants feel well-established and secure enough in their American identity to be free to become interested in the distinctive elements in their own heritage again, in contrast to their fathers who were more anxious to assert their full membership of the American community. It is doubtful whether this has provided much of an explanation for the remarkable post-war ecclesiastical prosperity of the USA, since it applied only to relatively recent immigrant groups, and perhaps most obviously to the Jewish community which Professor Herberg knows best.[21] But he was calling attention to a significant development, and the fact that such a process takes place is a reminder of how people's deepest loyalties and convictions can be overlaid and crowded out by more immediate interests for quite long periods and then reassert themselves with great force when circumstances change. Perhaps it is only in the early stages of new prosperity, and when people are also insecure about their status in society, that people strive to keep up with the Joneses. That phrase itself derives significantly from the surburban life of developing America.

Once they have all that the Joneses have, the search for more gadgets begins to lose its savour and the triviality of a life dedicated to their acquisition to be more apparent. Man needs bread, but he does not live by bread alone, especially when bread is in such easy supply as it is in the developed world today. In an age like the present, when many people are introspective and worried about their identity but seem to lack the courage to break new ground with a fresh commitment, the likelihood is that they will fall back on the most familiar and the most durable ideals of the past, those of nationality and religion. If decisive proof of this were needed, the extraordinary revival of these among the most reflective people of Eastern Europe, where the most determined and sustained efforts have been made to establish a society based on different ideals, provides it.

This is still a living issue and it is likely to become more and not less prominent as time goes on. The present anti-historical fashion does not go deep and it will soon pass. The British, of all people, cannot set aside their history. Nearly all of their instincts prompt them to define their future in relation to their understanding of their past, perhaps excessively in many instances. This will become increasingly obvious as the wider political and cultural implications of entry into the European Economic Community work themselves out. Unless they are dealt with in the light of a fresh interpretation of history, we shall at best muddle through in an unimaginative way, missing opportunities which are there for the taking, as we so often do, or we shall not get through at all. If that happens, we shall find ourselves at odds both with each other and with our new partners because we have not allowed for the pull of ancestral loyalties which have a way of asserting themselves very strongly when a radically new adjustment is called for. This is why they need to be looked at afresh today.

To say this is not necessarily to argue for the rehabilitation of these loyalties in their traditional form. Nor is it to prejudge where this re-examination might lead. The theologian, of all men, should be vigilant to show great caution and reserve in this matter, not least because theologians, and perhaps even more official ecclesiastical spokesmen, have not always been notable for showing such qualities in the past. Their occupational temptation, that of claiming divine authority over matters where they have no special competence, generally makes itself very strongly felt in this instance, especially in times of crisis, just because the connection between national identity and religious consciousness is so close. This is one of the places, therefore, where the theologian should start with an attitude of what Professor Donald MacKinnon has described in another context as 'reverent empiricism', laced with a healthy dash of frank agnosticism. Nations exist, and with them a strong sense of national identity. They have not always existed in their present form and there is no reason to suppose that they will not change again. We can see various historical reasons why they exist but are not given any theological reasons, except in the special case of the old Israel. The reasons there given throw into relief the relative, this-worldly character of all human organizations, including those where religious consciousness is bound up with a sense of national identity, and they provide little justification for a claim that any particular national consciousness has a peculiar status in the sight of God.

To say this, in its turn, is not to imply that a nation is necessarily a bad thing. On the contrary, if the theologian has any distinctive insight to offer in this field at all, it lies in the clarity with which he sees how ambiguous all forms of national organizations are, in their good and in their evil. This was superbly expressed by Reinhold Niebuhr in his *Structure of Nations and Empires*[22] and in many other works. As against both the fervent nationalist and the fervent anti-nationalist, he will hold fast to the simple facts that nations are inescapably there, that they have to be dealt with and that they are nearly all likely to have good and bad elements in them.

Obvious to the point of banality as that statement may be, what it says needs to be borne in mind when dealing with such an explosive subject as that of nationality, and the present situation provides no exception. It has three important implications.

First, a developed national consciousness is worthy of great respect because it represents a considerable achievement of civilization. Such a consciousness is not, of course, to be identified with nationalism, which is a political ideology that endeavours to express it. It has come into existence, generally over a long period, because people living close to each other have developed a strong sense of corporate identity and solidarity, so that they want to co-operate with one another. Usually, although by no means invariably, it is bound up with attachment to a particular place, which people have come to love and call their own, where they have built a common culture and brought up many generations of children to share a common heritage. Through acknowledged obligations expressed in laws and institutions, they have been trained to live together and care for each other as, in effect, members of one extended family.

These very basic facts need to be recalled in the face of the recrudescence of extremely naive thinking about society in our time, not least in universities where people might reasonably be expected to know better. History makes it painfully clear that the emergence of independent nations was far from being an unmixed blessing, yet it was not an unmixed curse either. The same is likely to be true in the case of new nations which are asserting their independent identity so aggressively in the world today. Patriotism as a slogan may well be the last refuge of a scoundrel, but genuine love of those who are nearest to one and share one's life, whether in the natural family or in the wider community, is the very basis of civilized responsibility. If a man cannot love his own kith and kin whom he sees, how can he love the international community, or for that matter the universal church, which he does not see? When white Americans alienated from their own society speak of themselves as 'white negroes', they are rightly viewed with suspicion by black people, who conclude that this apparent gesture of white solidarity with them owes more to hatred of other white people than to any real affection for themselves.

Many of the things which are often most admired by people who are acutely critical of nationality only became possible because of the strong sense of identity and mutual responsibility created by national feelings. The elaborate network of social services and, especially, a public system of education would never have developed without the existence of a state establishment which is infused with something like family feeling, that is, a nation. A national tradition also provides a manageable medium through which the human heritage can be passed on. No one can take it all in at once. To have a tradition of one's own is probably necessary before one can learn how to respect and appreciate those of others. The patriotic Briton who has managed to avoid xenophobia, rather than the committed servant of an ideology which is impatient of all national distinctions, is the person most likely to understand, and therefore allow for, the point of view of other nations, even in situations where their interests clash.

National feeling is a considerable achievement of civilization but, secondly, it is never good without qualification and its claims can never be absolute. It is strictly relative to greater loyalties, to God and to wider and more inclusive groupings of mankind. Problems always arise because, to the extent to which a nation becomes successful and a strong sense of national identity succeeds in expressing and institutionalizing itself, strong pressures to absolutize it build up. This is why national movements so quickly become self-justifyingly ideological. Just because of the closeness of the connection between the two and because of religious preoccupation with absolute standards and sanctions, the nation's religion lies ready to hand to be used for this purpose, with consequences only too depressingly familiar from the history of many nations. This is why any Christian who becomes deeply involved with the official life of a nation, or with the affairs of a nationalistic movement, and who becomes convinced of the rightness of its cause, has an obligation to be vigilantly self-critical and under no illusions concerning the difficulty of being honest about his situation. The test of his good faith will not lie in the protestations he makes of his own sincerity, or the degree of support which he finds among his allies, but in the amount of justice he is able to see in the position of those who seem to stand in the way of the realization of his nation's aims. His trust is in God, who is over and beyond the nations and the churches, including his own nation and church, and he needs especially to remember the transcendent nature of God when the interests of his nation and his church appear to coincide. Paganism originally arose as the worship of the gods of hearth and home, and paganism of this kind is the peculiar temptation of religious people, because good hearths and homes deserve to be cherished and the natural piety of religious people leads them to love them dearly. This is why, from Abraham onwards, the Bible reserves its sternest warnings for those who are in danger of surrendering to this particular temptation.

It follows from this, thirdly, that there must always be tension between national loyalty and religious commitment. Where there is no consciousness of tension, someone is being unfaithful. Two dangers, in particular, seem to be quite inescapable, so that they have always to be faced by those who are honest with themselves. On the one hand, members of strong nations find it hard not to believe that they have a prescriptive right to dictate the terms of their relationship to weaker nations. It is disconcerting that this difficulty often seems to be intensified when strong nations have been accustomed to thinking of themselves as Christian nations, especially when the weaker nations with whom they have been dealing have not. In such situations, they have to make a very great effort to remember that it is the 'meek', those of gentle spirit, who will alone inherit the earth. This means that the strong have to struggle to discover the distinctiveness of the other nations and so to deal with them that they are left with genuine freedom to express their own identity in ways which seem legitimate to themselves. There remains, of course, the possibility that their interests will still clash and have to be sorted out in relation to each other but, at least, the stronger nation will have begun with the right approach to the matter. The other danger arises among the relatively weaker nations. It produces a similar self-righteousness, but from the other end. Weaker nations have the moral satisfaction of being able to point out the faults of the stronger nations with which they are in contact and can readily go on to assume that the possibilities of righteousness in their situation are exhausted by their efforts to gain what they believe to be their due from the stronger nations. In the process they run the danger of losing all that is positive, and enriching to the whole, in their own sense of individuality by allowing their identity to be defined only in terms of their resentment of the greater strength of their neighbours. Those who are in such a situation will remember, in their turn, that the only safe rule for the Christian, whatever his material circumstances may be relatively to others, is to identify himself with the rich man in the gospel, who enjoys the heritage of the heirs of God's kingdom and with it all the temptation of riches. To the extent that he enjoys the inner freedom which comes from a genuine discovery of identity, he will be able to see that the same applies to his nation also.

It is only thus that the pride of power and the indignant self-righteousness which arises out of weakness can both be set in the context of the divine forbearance and stand any chance of being removed. To make one's heritage, whether national or ecclesiastical or both, a justification for either bullying or resentment, is to take away the virtue of the heritage itself and to surrender the possibility of being able to commend it to others as something they can respect and admire and partly adopt for themselves. If one is fortunate enough to have a national, or an ecclesiastical, heritage, of which one is proud, the right attitude is to cherish it gratefully as a gift and to offer a share in what can be made available of it to others with the modesty, eagerness to give pleasure and openness of spirit with which a gift is properly presented. This will make it easy for others to receive it with equal pleasure, because they will then feel honoured and enriched by its possession. Christians of all people should understand how relations between nations, as between churches, should strive to reflect that mutual dependence of the members of the body which Paul works out so fully in the twelfth chapter of the First Letter to the Corinthians.

This is the context in which the ecumenical movement in the Christian community should be understood. That movement is now more than one generation old and it has inevitably had to concentrate much of its attention, at least in Western lands, on the internal relations of churches to each other. There needs to be a reassertion that, as its founders saw very clearly, it is meant to be concerned with reconciliation between peoples as well as churches.[23] The chief reason why it is so concerned with the reunion of churches is that this is a way to make churches more representative of the way in which the whole human family is meant to be united before God. The word 'ecumenical' derives from the Greek word *oikumene*, which originally referred to the inhabited earth, the whole human set-up as known at that time. To act ecumenically, therefore, is not simply a matter of having dealings with members of other churches. It means to act in one's own situation with a sense of responsibility to God's unitive purpose for all his children. The primary ecumenical realities in the church are not the movements and organizations of church co-operation, which are very little different from any other movements and organizations, but the Bible, the gospel sacraments, the gifts of ministry and the great body of Christian tradition and experience throughout the ages which are available to all people. It is these alone, just because they point people beyond themselves and their own national and religious traditions and keep before them the Christian hope which calls them forward out of their settled local and sectarian ways into new experience, which make the overcoming of divisions possible.

Two implications follow for our present argument. First, the ecumenical movement is as much concerned with the quality of the internal life of individual churches and denominations and the attitudes they engender in their own members in dealing with each other and the wider community in which they are set as it is with relations between churches. Are their horizons being enlarged or are they contracting? It will be important to remember this when we come to consider the role which churches which have traditionally held a position of dominance within their own community should be playing in these communities today. Secondly, it should be frankly recognized that social and cultural issues are entirely proper, and indeed inescapable, subjects of ecumenical concern. No Christian at this time of day can consider questions of nationality, as they affect either church situations themselves or any other institutions, except in an ecumenical context. This does not necessarily imply rejection of any particular national loyalty, any more than ecumenical faithfulness necessarily involves repudiation of one's own church traditions. What it does mean is that the loyalty must be looked at in the setting of a wider loyalty, one which is shared with people who have a different national allegiance. Only thus can it be seen aright.

NOTES

1. Ian Nairn, *London*, Penguin Books 1966, pp. 18f.
2. Wynford Vaughan Thomas and Alun Llewellyn, *The Shell Guide to Wales*, Michael Joseph 1969, p. 167, in writing about the birthplace of George Herbert in Montgomery, argue that the quality of quick transference of thought and controlled and concentrated passion of metaphysical poetry is distinctively Welsh, citing the complex, tightly disciplined nature of the Welsh poetic structure and the Welsh origins of Herbert, Vaughan and Donne in justification. To claim this quality as *distinctively* Welsh is to claim too much, but the Welsh influence is manifest.
3. See A. R. Vidler, *The Orb and the Cross*, Longman 1945.
4. Salvador de Madariaga, *Englishmen, Frenchmen, Spaniards*, 1928, 2nd ed., Pitman 1970; Ernest Barker, *National Character and the Factors in its Formation*, Methuen 1927.
5. G. Santayana, *Soliloquies in England*, Constable 1937.
6. D. Brogan, *The English People*, Hamish Hamilton 1943.
7. George Orwell, *The English People*, Collins 1947. It also showed the only too typically Etonian preference for ignoring the existence of the large upper-working-class sections of the community, who merge easily with the lower-middle class.
8. A. L. Morton, *The Matter of Britain*, Lawrence and Wishart 1966.
9. A. L. Rowse, *The English Spirit*, Macmillan 1966.
10. G. Kitson Clark, *The English Inheritance*, SCM Press 1950.
11. Geoffrey Ashe, *Camelot the Vision of Albion*, Heinemann 1971.
12. Charles Williams, *Taliessin through Logres*, Oxford University Press 1938; *The Region of the Summer Stars*, Nicholson and Watson 1944. See also his *Arthurian Torso*, ed. C. S. Lewis, Oxford University Press 1948, and Lewis's essay 'Williams and the Arthuriad', op. cit., p. 93.
13. David Jones, *Anathemata*, Faber 1952, p. 11.
14. *Royal Commission on the Constitution, 1969–1973*, Vols I & II, HMSO 1973 (Kilbrandon Report).
15. *Commission on the Constitution* I, para. 61.
16. Even this, however, has been at the price of a loss of organic connection with other loyalties, such as that to one's neighbourhood or country. Thus Manchester United were able to draw on widespread national support in the 1960s which would have been inconceivable previously.
17. James McMillan, *The Anatomy of Scotland*, Leslie Frewin 1969, p. 31.
18. See Charles H. Anderson, *White Protestant Americans: From National Origins to Religious Groups*, Prentice-Hall, Englewood Cliffs

1970, which demonstrates how American Lutherans of Swedish extraction retain their Lutheranism very firmly while identifying themselves fully with American life.

19. Before the Kilbrandon Report appeared, I had already been surprised at the number and vehemence of the expressions of Yorkshire, Lancashire or more general 'Northern' self-consciousness that I have overheard in bars and trains and common rooms. This impression is confirmed by the Attitude Survey for the Royal Commission on the Constitution, 1969–1973, and quoted in the Memorandum of Dissent: 'A major finding is that feelings of regional identity are strong throughout the country. Although they are particularly strong in Wales and Scotland, they are almost as marked in the South West and Yorkshire' (Vol. II, para. 46).

20. Will Herberg, *Protestant-Catholic-Jew*, Doubleday, New York 1955.

21. Its relevance event to these has recently been challenged by Stephen Sharot, 'The Three-Generation Thesis and the American Jew', *British Journal of Sociology* XXIV, June 1973, pp. 151–64f. A recent article in the US government publication *Insight USA* has claimed, however, that this process of 're-ethnicization' has recently taken on a new lease of life, although not necessarily or only in religious forms: see John Stirn and William H. Stringer, 'The Re-ethnicization Game', *Insight USA*, September 1973.

22. Reinhold Niebuhr, *The Structure of Nations and Empires*, Scribner, New York 1959. It is impossible to read that book today without bitter regret that its message was not heeded by American policy-makers in relation to the Far East in the sixties.

23. This has been forcibly restated, with ample historical verification, in the recent lectures of Dr W. A. Visser 't Hooft, *Has the Ecumenical Movement a Future?*, Christian Journals, Belfast 1974, pp. 76–83.

*   *   *

Since the words about modern American scholars (p. 7 above) were written, such an American work has appeared, *Internal Colonialism: the Celtic Fringe in British National Development, 1536–1966*, by Michael Hechter, Routledge and Kegan Paul 1975. See my review of it in *New Society*, 10 July 1975 (Vol. 33, No. 666).

II

THE MATTER OF SCOTLAND

English people, as we have seen, are rarely prepared fully to admit the extent to which Britain is inhabited by different nations. They will agree that Ireland is different but, for all practical purposes, they prefer to take being Scottish or Welsh as slightly deviant and humorous, and perhaps slightly inferior, ways of being English. This is a serious error. Unless English people appreciate the extent of the error,[1] the nature of the links which bind the Scots and Welsh to the English in one united kingdom is misunderstood, and therefore their strength is weakened. It is not simply that Scottish and Welsh nationalities have a different sentiment attached to them, which must be respected because Scots and Welsh are apt to be touchy. It is that these are genuinely different people, with differing histories, institutions and cultural styles from the English. This comes out clearly in church life, but it is true over a much wider field. Welsh institutions have been assimilated to those of England more than those of Scotland have, but the Welsh system of kinship remains significantly different. It would be naive to say that the Welsh have no class-consciousness, as some of their spokesmen claim, but it is true that, except in the most Anglicized parts of the country, the value given to class differences is very different from what it is in England.[2] Similarly, the differences between the Scots legal and educational systems and those of England are well known, but there are other more pervasive differences. In many parts of Scotland, the attitude to renting and buying houses is quite different from that in England, even among those who would be considered in English terms to belong to the middle classes.[3] The priorities in news-value in the *Scotsman* newspaper in Edinburgh are sharply different from those in the London *Times* and they are not merely those of a local as compared with a national newspaper. They are those of a paper which serves a different nation.

Even relatively enlightened Englishmen can be heard to express the view that, if there is a difference between England and the 'Celtic fringe', a revealing inaccuracy, it is only that the latter is a generation behind the former in responding to trends which operate in the great world. This is as insensitive as it is complacent. It is only partially true even on the superficial level where it might be held to have a measure of plausibility, that of popular fashion and the spread of those things on which the public media of communication concentrate. Cardiff is not far behind London in feminine dress sense, and not only was Edinburgh the first post-war city to organize a major international festival of the arts, but Glasgow Celtic were also the first British team to win the European Cup. But it is very wide of the mark in relation to more fundamental matters. The acids of modernity do their corrosive work everywhere, and they are busy in Aberdeen and Swansea as they are in London, but they operate on different kinds of material and with varying degrees of density of pollution. The possibility cannot be ruled out that granite and slate are proving more resistant to them than brick and stucco. If so, only those who take a decadent pleasure in observing the process of corrosion will regard this as a sign of backwardness.

While the differences between England and Scotland are far from being only differences in dominant religious allegiance, it remains true that these differences come out sharply in this sphere. There are solid historical reasons for this,[4] but it is by no means a matter of merely historical interest. This came out very clearly in the controversy aroused not so long ago about the appearance of the so-called 'Bishops' Report', the report of a commission of enquiry of English and Scots churchmen appointed to examine conditions in which intercommunion between the Church of

England and the Church of Scotland might become possible.[5]
Most Englishmen, including many fairly devout Englishmen, are
probably unaware of the existence of this report. Very few Scots,
including many not at all devout, will be without some knowledge
of it, even if they know of it only through tendentious accounts in
the *Scottish Daily Express*, which ran a violent campaign against it
of a kind which would have been inconceivable in its London
counterpart. Its apparently innocuous proposals that the Scottish
Kirk should take episcopacy into its system, of which more later,
were seen by the Scots at the time as a threat to their distinctive
identity, as yet another take-over bid of Scottish institutions by
their English rival, and this time the one which was the very shrine
of their nationhood. The story was often repeated at the time of the
Scottish journalist in London who was heard to fulminate against
the proposals of the report. A bewildered English colleague asked
him why he was getting so excited, since he was an atheist anyway.
The reply was, 'An atheist maybe, but a Presbyterian atheist.' It is
doubtful whether, in a similar situation, the reaction of David
Hume himself would have been very different.

Most English people realize that it is the Presbyterian and not
the Anglican church which is established in Scotland, yet few of
them realize how different the relationship is both to state and
nation.[6] To begin with, the Church of Scotland is far more firmly
rooted in the life of the community than is the Church of England,
and people identify themselves with it far more closely. The
Church of England may enshrine a great deal of English history,
but the Church of Scotland is also a major factor in present-day
Scottish life. The most cursory examination of the *Church of
Scotland Year Book* will confirm the truth of this. What immediately
strikes an English reader is the enormously impressive institutional
stability of the Kirk in the modern world. It is true that it has
suffered in all the changes which have overtaken Britain, including
Scotland, in recent times. The Kirk is weaker than it was, but the
decline in membership over the last fifty years is small as compared
with the massive attrition which has overtaken both the Church of
England and the Free Churches in the same period. In his
careful studies of the Church of Scotland, Dr John Highet

of Glasgow University showed that two out of three people in
Scotland in the 1950s belonged to churches and attended services
with relative regularity.[7] The proportion will be lower now, but it
will still be substantially higher than the English proportion.
Among those who do attend church, also, the average level of
commitment seems to be higher, even though it is doubtful
whether the difference is as great among the hard core of those
most deeply committed. This is proved quite concretely by the
statistics which the *Year Book* provides of 'Christian Liberality',
to quote the engaging term which the Scots use to describe the
financial contributions of members to the work of their churches.
These indicate that the average Scot must give to the church far
more than the average member of an Anglican electoral roll and
nearly as much as the average member of an English Free Church.
Both these latter groups together add up to a much smaller
proportion of the population of their country than the members of
the Church of Scotland.

What is more significant for the influence of the church on
ordinary life is that the existence of the office of eldership within
the Presbyterian system means that a far larger number of people
who are not professional clergymen are involved with the pastoral
work and administration of the church than is the case in England.
There is no real English parallel to this situation. It is true that
churchwardens and lay members of synods in the Church of
England and lay preachers in Methodism and elders and deacons
in other Free Churches have not dissimilar functions, but they are
far fewer in relation to the rest of the population. Some large
Scottish congregations will have several dozen elders and most
have a substantial number.[8] Not many of them can escape relatively onerous obligations. The social effect of having so many
leading members of ordinary communities, about 48,000 all told,
with such a well-defined ecclesiastical role in relation to such large
numbers of their neighbours, must be considerable, and it makes
an important difference between Scottish and English life.

Finally, it is very striking that church membership appears to be
almost as strong in cities and industrial areas as it is in suburbs,
seaside resorts and the countryside.[9] The strength of the church in

industrial areas remains remarkable by English standards, and
indeed by those of most other heavily industrialized countries. Nor
does this membership appear to be merely formal since, again by
this very specific test, the 'Christian Liberality' of congregations in
these areas holds up reasonably well as compared with the others.
Linked with this, again in strong contrast to England, if not so
much to Wales and Ireland, manual workers as well as 'white-
collar' workers are to be found in large numbers in the church.[10]
In Scotland, as in most other places, it is broadly true that the
more professional and middle-class a neighbourhood is, the
stronger its church is likely to be, but the disparity is nothing like
so great as it is in England. The contrast in church-going between,
say, Motherwell and Barnsley, or Paisley and Halifax, or Kil-
marnock and Nuneaton, to take roughly comparable communities,
is startling. Nor can this be accounted for on the ground that the
Scots are more set in their ways than the English and have not felt
the impact of mobility so strongly. The contrast between church-
going in the new town of East Kilbride outside Glasgow and that
in, say, Basildon, outside London, is even more startling.

Partly because of this difference in the degree and quality of
popular support they enjoy, as well as because of the accident of
history which made the church the main repository of the national
consciousness in Scotland after 1707, the relation of the two
national churches to the matter of their respective national
identities is also different. While it is undeniable that Anglicanism
is an important element in the English tradition, it would be hard
for any one to maintain that it was the decisive one, or, at least,
anyone who tried to do so would have to recognize that this was not
a view shared by the majority of his fellow Englishmen or even of
his fellow Anglicans. But in Scotland, the majority of people would
probably still take this view. It is true that sizeable minorities
might not. The Episcopal Church in Scotland bitterly resents being
called 'The English Church', as it still is in some parts of Scotland,
since it claims more continuity with some aspects of medieval
Scotland than the Kirk. And while many of the large numbers of
Scottish Roman Catholics retain Irish connections and loyalties,[11]
there is enough indigenous Catholicism to make it a significant

strain in the national life. Many Scottish Catholics are, in fact, fervent Scots nationalists. The influence of the legal system, also, although not as pervasive as that of the Kirk, is no less distinctive of the nation and, in Edinburgh at least, is equally important as a factor in defining the national identity. The same is also partly true, although much modified since the nineteenth century, of Scottish education and medicine.

Yet when all these qualifications have been made, it remains true that the Church of Scotland is a major focus of the national consciousness and the main custodian of the national heritage. This becomes manifest almost to the point of being oppressive at the time of the General Assembly in May when, as they never weary of reminding each other, this gathering of churchmen becomes the nearest thing to a national parliament that Scotland possesses. The official committees of the General Synod (the former Church Assembly) of the Church of England, and of the British Council of Churches, have long had pertinent things to say about national affairs, but they do not command the same attention nor do they speak with the self-confidence born of the knowledge of their representative character as does the famous Church and Nation committee of the Church of Scotland which, over the years, has produced a sustained running commentary on the 'state of the nation' which has no parallel in the rest of Christendom. How far this self-confidence is justified any longer is an open question. Modern Scotland is no longer 'the parish hall of the Kirk' and, as in Wales, the utterances of ministers carry nothing like the weight nor command the same degree of public attention that they did even within living memory. It is still true, however, that the Church of Scotland is much less on the margin of the life of the average Scot than the Church of England and the Free Churches are on the life of the average Englishman. Not only is the Scot more likely to be in church on Sunday and more ready to support the church with his contributions but, even when he is not, he is more likely to know the minister personally and to have some opinion concerning his preaching ability. It is inconceivable in England that any clergyman, however often he might appear on television, could call at a pub and not be allowed by the landlord to leave until he had shaken hands personally with everyone in the bar, as happened as recently as the 1960s with Professor William Barclay near Glasgow. The church still counts as a very important element in the ordinary community life of Scotland.

The answer to the question of how far that influence has been beneficent will obviously depend largely on the preconceptions of the observer. But it should also depend on a knowledge of Scottish history and an awareness of what the alternatives might have been. Thus the notes of grimness and harshness in Scottish life have both been exaggerated in themselves by currently fashionable hedonism and also attributed to Scottish religion when they may just as easily come into the religion from another source. As that perceptive observer of Scottish life, Ian Finlay, once remarked, we hear a great deal of what Calvinism did to Scotland but do not hear so much of what Scotland did to Calvinism. When Calvinism opens out into the wider world, as it has in Holland and Switzerland and eastern America, as well as in Lowland Scotland, it generally wears a kindlier face than ill-informed modern prejudice is prepared to admit. It is when its exponents live in an isolated community which distrusts its neighbours and becomes fearful for the integrity of its own way of life, as in South Africa and parts of the Highlands and Islands, that it turns in upon itself and becomes sour and self-righteous. In Scotland, the early Calvinism of the sixteenth century, as expressed in the great Confession of 1560, was more generous and imaginatively stimulating than that of the Covenanters of the seventeenth century, where real harshness and bigotry were involved. Even this grim self-discipline, however, has had its creative results in toughening the Scottish character. Would the sharp realism of David Hume, for example, have been possible without the long tradition of moral and intellectual rigour which preceded it? Could his work be thought of as the work of a more urbane secularized Covenanter protesting against the increasing sentimentality of a Moderatism which wanted to have it both ways without honestly facing the implications either of Christian faith or of rationalistic enlightenment? Whatever answers may be given to these questions, they are a reminder of the dangers of reading history in over-simple terms and of the need to see that strong movements have an inescapable influence on those who inherit their traditions, even when they may appear to be repudiating them. The history of Scotland is as mixed as that of other nations, and the history of the Kirk in relation to Scotland is mixed, and it is important that those of us who live south of the border should be on our guard against reading it, and dismissing it, in terms of tired clichés which may reveal more about our own ignorance and complacency than about the actual situation.

This is put in such sharp terms because it matters a great deal in these days that those who live in the rest of these islands should go out of their way to emphasize that they appreciate something of the full magnitude of the Scottish achievement. Over the last two centuries, the Scots have shown themselves to be a great people, one of the greatest in the world. No small nation, with the possible exception of Switzerland, can point to a comparable body of achievement in so many different fields. For the English to regard the Scots as their poor relations, or for the weaker Scots, when they contemplate their problems, to water their whisky with self-pitying tears, is absurd. Scotland is no marginal hill-farm on the British estate. It is one of its most intensively cultivated and richest properties.

The success of Scotland has lain not merely in her ability to assert her own national identity and to maintain it over against outside threats, as a distinct province of Britain, but in her ability to contribute distinctively to the life of the world. Scotland over the last two centuries has proved herself to be one of the hearths of civilization.

Within Mackenzie's crowded life-time of eighty-six years [1745–1831], Scotland produced the greatest of sceptical philosophers, David Hume; the best loved of song poets, Robert Burns; the king of romancers, Sir Walter Scott; the two chief masters of modern biography, James Boswell and John Gibson Lockhart; the most virile of British portrait painters, Sir Henry Raeburn; the greatest British architect of his century, Robert Adam. At the same time, the dynasty of the Doctors Monro made Edinburgh's Medical College the most respected in the world; Adam Smith founded the modern science of Political Economy, James Hutton did as much for Geology, and Joseph Black revolutionized Chemistry. Nor was this all; the world's roads were rebuilt according to the methods of John Loudon McAdam; the world's industry was remade by the steam-engine of James Watt; the world's annals of military glory shone with new lustre at the exploits of the most famous of regiments, the Black Watch.[12]

The record of the Scots in the succeeding century is perhaps less spectacular, but is only a little less considerable.[13]

That the Scots have been very successful people in England has, of course, been a familiar fact for a long time, although its significance for the quality of British life has rarely been seen. What has not yet received as much attention, especially from the English, has been the extent of the Scottish achievement overseas.

All in all, the success of the Scots abroad was not exaggerated by Sir Charles Dilke when he wrote, 'In British settlements from Canada to Ceylon, from Dunedin to Bombay, for every Englishman you meet who had worked himself up to wealth from small beginnings without external aids, you find ten Scotsmen' (*Great Britain*, 1888, p. 525) . . . Whereas the Irishman crosses the sea in sorrow and despair, the Scot does so in calculated contentment . . .The Scotch immigrant is a man who leaves Scotland because he wishes to rise faster and higher than he can at home.[14]

One wonders whether this would have been true of many of the Highlanders who, as a result of the Clearances and for other reasons, left more in the spirit of the Irish, but it would seem to be fair enough as a description of the attitude of most Lowlanders. Nor was this merely a matter of the pursuit of material wealth. Vast numbers of Scots ministers and missionaries and teachers have gone overseas, often to situations of great hardship and peril, and have helped to set a Scottish stamp on developing communities. Although the Scots lost out through their loyalty to the Crown at the founding of the Republic, it is not often realized, for example, that their role in laying the foundations of American civilization, religion and education, was almost as great as that of New England, and perhaps even greater in the westward expansion of the nation.[15]

What merits special attention in the context of our argument is that the Scots seem to have won this success without incurring a tithe of the resentment which upper-class Englishmen aroused. The Scots abroad have been tenacious, and occasionally ruthless, enough in pursuing their own interests, but they have been largely free from that sense of automatic superiority and the 'habit of command' which afflicted the English.[16] They have a gift, even when they are in positions of authority, of relating themselves to people of other cultures in such a way that the others do not feel that their own identity is threatened. They themselves, in their turn, are able to take themselves for granted and not to feel in any danger of losing their own identity. This, as we shall see, is in marked contrast to the Welsh. There is, of course, a sub-culture of Scottish exiles, with its St Andrew's societies, Burns suppers, piping the haggis and sword-dancing, but this is hardly taken with real seriousness even by those who participate in it and there is little clannishness among the Scots abroad. It is nothing like the rich, warm and exclusive life of Welsh exiles. There are over thirty Welsh churches in and around London, with a full round of social activities associated with them, but there are only a few Scots churches and they are slightly apologetic about their separate existence, although there must be at least as many people in the London area who consider themselves Scots as there are Welsh. Again to quote Donaldson,

> The Scot, angular and rugged as he may be in his individuality, was often remarkably adaptable and ready to assimilate himself and conform to a new community in which he settled. And despite his heritage of bitter division on ecclesiastical and political issues at home, he could be remarkably tolerant of the ways of others. The egalitarianism of Scottish society helped Scots to accept peoples of various social backgrounds, and it has been suggested that the existence in Scotland of two races and two languages made Scots less sensitive than many Europeans to differences of race and colour and therefore readier to establish and maintain good relations with natives. It was certainly true that with their broader and less insular outlook than the English, they had the advantage that they did not regard all the ways of life other than their own as necessarily backward or barbarous.[17]

Quite apart from what Scots immigrants have done, Scotland at home has continued right up to our own time to export many of its distinctive products to an admiring world, and the more prosperous the world has become, the more desirable those products have seemed to be. This austere Presbyterian land has yet contrived to produce some of the most cherished luxury articles or activities, of which whisky, golf, high-quality woollen goods and beef are only the chief. The ultimate symbol of business success in modern Japan is to belong to a golf club and to have a bottle of Johnnie Walker Black Label —that and no other—on the table at the nineteenth hole. More seriously, Scots medical, engineering and farming skill continue to be in strong demand and, at least until very recently indeed, Scots theological learning and preaching. It was a famous American Methodist preacher who said, in an unexpected metaphor, that Scotsmen were the 'Chivas Regal of the American pulpit'. 'Made in Scotland' is probably the most envied stamp of quality to be found anywhere in the world.

What, then, are the distinctive qualities of Scotland which have given it such a reputation, and how are they related to the British way of living?

The first is Scottish moral seriousness. This is an unfashionable virtue in these nervously self-conscious days, when we are more aware of the dangers of making self-committing moral judgments than of their inescapable necessity, but this quality is the source of a great deal of Scottish strength, even if it may also lie near the root of some of the Scottish limitations. Scots people are less likely to take things easily and to hope to muddle through than are the English. They are remarkably free from the kind of sophistication, which may derive from the strong influence of the aristocracy in setting social standards in conventional English life, that regards it as a form of bad taste to be articulate about matters of principle and to state one's premises openly and be prepared to draw logical conclusions from them and then to argue their merits, leaving oneself open to be convinced by counter-arguments. The English view is much more that someone properly brought up should be able to take his principles for granted and instinctively know what to do in their light. To have something of this Scottish attitude is an enormous source of strength in a rapidly changing world. This quality of moral seriousness was exemplified very vividly in recent times by John Reith. The important thing to note about him was that, despite the sniggers which he provoked among the self-conscious people who abound in the world of communications and despite his own peculiar 'hang-ups', it was he who was strong enough to inject a bracing self-confidence into the BBC which enabled it to do such a splendid pioneering job in a field exceptionally full of pitfalls.

Secondly, this moral seriousness is closely related to a strong public sense. Scots are among the most 'inner-directed' of people, in David Riesman's phrase, and they may have a lively speculative interest, but they are not much interested in their own mental states. Scots are individuals, of course, and not types, and there are introverted Scots, especially among Highlanders, but they are not typical. The typical Scot of sound mind is more interested in his situation than in himself. This sometimes limits his artistic achievement, but helps him to have sound implements and institutions. Many Scots are accountants, and the notion of accountability lies deep in the Scottish attitudes. The Scot is not satisfied, as an Englishman might be, with the fact that something works. He wants it to make sense, so that he can justify it and know where to put his finger when something goes wrong. Thus the established Kirk of Scotland does not merely work. Anyone can quickly come to understand how it works, and opportunity is given for questions to be asked and for answers to be given when things do not work. Matters are dealt with, as they should be, decently and in order.

This sense of accountability is also related to the strong Scots conviction that things are improvable. The land and the climate do not encourage people to believe that rewards are easily obtainable, as they may be in some parts of England. The world is not naturally a garden, which needs only to be gently tended. It is a wilderness, which needs to be enclosed and drained and sheltered before it can be made to blossom as the rose. The Scots, above all people, are the great 'improvers', and in more senses than the agricultural. This may be bound up with that sense of 'calling' which Reformed Protestantism engenders and which, in some prominent Scots, becomes almost a sense of destiny, but which in ordinary solid Scots becomes a more prosaic acceptance of the duty of self-improvement and the improvement of society. This gives to the Lowland Scots that touch of austerity which is lacking, for example, in the Welsh who have a similar Protestant faith and, for that matter, in many Celtic Scots. By way of reaction also, this may also partly account for the particularly sordid and hopeless character of Scottish low life, as reflected in some of the Glasgow slums. If a man is not prepared to improve himself, it is a sentimental waste of time for others to try to do it for him. As a rough generalization, it can be said that while, over very large areas, there are few societies more decent and honourable than that of Scotland and few people more generous and compassionate to the genuinely unfortunate, the respectable Scot is, perhaps, a little less than tender to the shiftless and delinquent. The Scottish schoolmaster retains the use of the tawse, and it is the Glasgow police who appear to feel most strongly that capital punishment for murder should be restored.

Thirdly, because he is such a good mixer, like his national drink, the Scot has been an outstandingly good citizen of the world. He maintains his own unmistakable identity without needing to underline it and he is too 'inner-directed' to want to ingratiate himself with anybody, yet his practical competence makes him valuable to others, who are able to respect him without feeling that they have to alter their own lives except in relation to the matter in hand. As Professor Donaldson puts it,

> With all their successes in so many walks of life, the impression that the Scots have made on the new English-speaking nations has been curiously limited. They exported their ecclesiastical institutions, mainly for themselves, and they preserved, again mainly among themselves, many of the trappings of Scottish, and more particularly Highland, ways of life. But the law and civil institutions of nearly all the communities overseas are essentially English and are assuredly never Scottish. Here the Scots capacity for assimilation comes in; when transplanted from his homeland he finds no difficulty in accustoming himself to unfamiliar terms and institutions; he lives in towns which have 'mayors' and conducts his affairs according to a legal system in which every proceeding is the work of solicitors and the work of the judicature is radically different from those known in Scotland.[18]

This is a source of strength rather than weakness in the Scots attitude. In fact, it is possible to go further and risk incurring the wrath of nationalists by arguing that the unique virtues of the Scots become more visible as they move out from their homeland into a wider world than on their own hearth. The Scots virtues bound all together in the domestic life of the country do produce a rather heavy lump, which sometimes fails to rise. As an ingredient in the life of the wider community, they act as a precious leaven.

By this point in the discussion, an internal critic of Scots life may well be on the point of exploding. He will protest that this account of the Lowland Scot is ridiculously idealized, comparable in its sentimental dishonesty to that of the romantic Highlander of Victorian legend and the tourist trade. Whatever shreds of truth there may be of the picture of Scots in the past and in the wider world, he would argue that modern Scotland is nothing more than a provincial backwater, second-rate and infinitely complacent in its second-ratedness. If Scotland did once lead the world in education and ideas, that lead has long since vanished in the mists of the past. Her church is narcissistic and smugly old-fashioned, wavering between a dull prosiness and nostalgic sentimentality. In what other country in the world, except perhaps for the Scottish parts of Canada and New Zealand, could a university professor, like the Dr William Barclay already mentioned, get away with shamelessly trotting out as though they were newly-minted the most hackneyed sermon illustrations of two generations and calling it a lecture, while admiring television audiences lap it up? Ordinary Scottish life is barren of quality, but the Scots are far less self-critical than the English, just because the English cannot escape the winds which blow through the great world so easily. The typical Scots scene is that of a family sitting around a tea-table laden with more starch than is good for them, presided over by a matron of invincible self-satisfaction who has just finished a cosy book by O. Douglas or Annie S. Swan, while the Glasgow Orpheus Choir sing slowly in the background, loading every syllable of 'Crimond' with a double helping of treacle. For all his alleged theological interest, the real god of the Scot is a safe and stodgy conventionality, and his enemy is anyone who disturbs his complacency with a new idea.

No doubt there is a good deal of justice in such a tirade. There is much small-minded complacency in modern Scotland, which can easily lie behind loyalty to the Scottish heritage and disapproval of many aspects of the modern world, and not a little spurious religiosity. Hugh Ross Mackintosh, a shrewd professor of theology of unquestioned Scots loyalty, once said in my hearing many years ago that a good friend of his who knew the place intimately used to allege that there were no more than four genuinely committed Christians in a prosperous golfing community outside Edinburgh where churchgoing was well up to average. Yet impatient internal critics, acutely concious of their country's weakness and eager to reform them, are not necessarily the most balanced judges of its quality. Like the restless children of a good family, who are naturally eager to break out and explore wider horizons, they may take for granted what outsiders recognize as distinctive and precious. Like all other countries, Scotland has its dark side, and more than some others, it has its dull side. Scotland badly needs to refresh her ideal of her task among the nations and to do so with reference to factors outside as well as within her own life. Yet, as Britain moves into the larger European community, no part of these islands, proportionately to its size, has more to give to the enrichment of her future life than Scotland, and Scotland will be failing in her duty to Britain unless she sees this and acts upon it.

That last sentence may strike very curiously on many Scottish ears, and that this should be so points to what is most seriously wrong in the attitude of many Scotsmen. For too long, Scotland as a nation has found it convenient to hide behind the size and dominating position of the English as a way of evading the need to measure up to its own international responsibilities, both within and beyond these islands. This has been bad for Scotland and bad for Britain. In a world which needs all the strength it can get, Scotland provides a position of strength from which many people have sallied forth in the past to the great benefit of others. They are needed today as much as they ever were. Like anywhere else, Scotland has its own special problems, such as those of Clydeside and the depopulation of the Highlands and Islands, but it is ridiculous to think of Scotland as a whole as any kind of distressed area. There may be too much dreary Scottish provincialism, but it is no more dreary and no more provincial that that of industrial and rural England, and the great institutions of Scotland are not in the least provincial. Edinburgh is a worthy capital, which has undergone a considerable renaissance since the war, and it is the modish triviality of visiting London critics rather than the sober judgment of its citizens which stands exposed before the world at Festival time. The Scottish universities, in sharp contrast to the University of Wales and most of the regional English universities, are both genuinely Scottish and genuinely international. Few people could have exemplified both these characteristics more clearly than the late Lord Boyd Orr. The Church of Scotland badly needs to open a few more windows and have a breath of fresh air blowing through it, but even its sternest critics would hardly argue that it needs root and branch reformation.

One of the most refreshing things which has happened to Scotland over the last generation has been the Iona Community. It did open a few windows in a genuine effort to renew the vision of the Scottish church, and through it the Scottish nation. There may have been an element of romanticism about its policy, as there has been about the personality of its very attractive founder, but that has added an agreeable touch of colour to what is often a drab enough scene, and most of its activities have kept very close to the ground of life in modern Scotland. Yet it is no disparagement of the Iona Community to say what many Scotsmen who also greatly admire its work themselves feel, that it does not represent Scotland at its characteristic best. It is good to recall the gentle heritage of the Celtic church and to set it against the dourness of the Covenanting tradition, but Scotland at her best is a country which is more interested in the future than the past. Let England cherish her continuity with the past. She has made a business of it for long enough and has learnt to be better at it than Scotland. Scotland is a country of the Reformed kind, one which looks forward and outward, to improve and to innovate. Any covenant her members enter must be one which builds for the future, not one which tries to reconstitute or embalm the past. There is still plenty of work for Scotsmen to do in the world and it is time they got on with it.

This is not to deny that Scotland needs to give due attention, in an age of centralization and standardization, to the maintenance and strengthening of her own hearth nor that, along with Wales, she has a claim on the sympathy and co-operation of England and her own scattered children overseas in doing so. Yet experience proves that even that hearth itself is best preserved by being thrown open to the influence of the wider world. North Sea oil and the development of Edinburgh's influential financial expertise may do as much for the preservation of Scottish identity as shipbuilding and the reputation of Edinburgh University did in the last century and much more than any backward-looking political programmes. The tower of Paisley Abbey is clearly visible from Glasgow's new airport, and that is as it should be in Scotland. The faith of the Reformation, when left to turn in upon itself, either goes soft and sentimental or rigidly defensive, and it does so particularly obviously in Scotland because it so completely denies that aspect of it which Scotland has exemplified more clearly than almost any other country. It is strength and not weakness which drives Christian faith into the wider world, and that is supremely true of the Scottish character as framed by that faith. No country needs to worry less about problems of national identity than Scotland. Let her take up again her calling of providing expert service for the rest of the world and, losing her life without making too much of a fuss about what she is doing, she will continue to find it. What this might mean for the internal relations of the different peoples in these islands will be the theme of a later section.

NOTES

1. As the Kilbrandon Report says, 'Although there is no ill-will or intended discourtesy in this attitude of the English, people in Scotland and Wales are much irritated by it. It fails to recognize the special character of their separate identity, of which they themselves are keenly conscious and proud; and at the same time it implies that the resentment they feel arises only because they are living in the past and getting agitated about something which is no longer important' (Vol. I, para. 332, p. 103).

2. This is demonstrated, along with other subtle differences, in P. J. Madgwick (with N. Griffiths and V. Walker), *The Politics of Rural Wales: A Study of Cardiganshire*, Hutchinson 1973.

3. P. L. Sissons, *The Social Significance of Church Relationships in the Borough of Falkirk*, Church of Scotland 1973, p. 35.

4. How this came to be as the result of the Act of Union and how, for a variety of reasons, the church was able only imperfectly to fulfil its role at the centre of the national culture is shown with great clarity and refreshing objectivity in David Daiches' Whidden Lectures, *The Paradox of Scottish Culture*, Oxford University Press 1964.

5. *Relations between Anglican and Presbyterian Churches: a Joint Report*, SPCK 1957.

6. This is even more true of modern Ireland, as is made startlingly clear by J. L. Whyte, *Church and State in Modern Ireland, 1922–1970*, Gill and Macdonald 1971.

7. John Highet, *Churches in Scotland Today*, Jackson 1950; id., *The Scottish Churches Churches 400 Years after the Reformation*, Skeffington 1960.

8. It was one of the weaknesses of the famous Bishops' Report that it underestimated the extent of this difference. On the face of it, its recommendation that the Church of England should take the eldership into its system and that the Church of Scotland should adopt episcopacy might seem reasonable enough, but it was never a starter at all. As the event showed, to ask the Scots, given their history, to accept bishops was asking more than many of them were prepared to give, but the deafening silence which greeted the proposal that the Church of England should adopt the eldership, a silence which has remained virtually unbroken to this day, indicates the complete lack of realism of the proposal. The Church of England, of all bodies, was to be required to ordain tens of thousands of people to a new office, with no tradition in Anglican life to guide them and with a prejudice against it as something Scottish and Presbyterian. Could anyone honestly have supposed that a typical member of a Parochial Church Council or the Mother's Union would contemplate becoming an elder?

9. It is true that statistics can sometime mislead here, since it is still customary in parts of the Highlands for people who are diligent in church attendance not to commit themselves to full church membership until they are safely near the end of their lives.

10. This is confirmed by P. L. Sissons' recent study of Falkirk referred to in note 3 above. It is true that the leadership of the church even in an industrial town like Falkirk is largely middle-class, and that skilled manual workers are more numerous in churches, especially the Church of Scotland, than unskilled manual workers, but this remains a very different situation from that obtaining in most parts of England.

11. It is not often realized that much of the savagery in the rivalry between Rangers and Celtic football supporters derives from their being the descendants of Ulster immigrants who carry on their Irish feuds on foreign soil.

12. Harold W. Thompson, *A Scottish Man of Feeling*, Oxford University Press 1931, p. 1. David Daiches, *The Paradox of Scottish Culture*, p. 74, after quoting this exuberant outpouring, goes on to qualify it by pointing out that all these do not add up to the manifestation of a national culture. That may well be true, but from the point of view of this book, that makes it the more impressive. These are great human achievements, internationally relevant.

13. Thus, Scots born in the nineteenth century claim to have invented the bicycle, pneumatic tyre, gas lighting, the rubber waterproof, refrigeration and television, not to mention penicillin and anaesthetics. See James McMillan, *The Anatomy of Scotland*, p. 199.

14. Gordon Donaldson, *The Scots Overseas*, Robert Hale 1966, pp. 205f.

15. See Ian Charles Cargill Graham, *Colonists from Scotland*, Cornell University Press 1956.

16. Unless they were the kind of Scots brought up in English schools or otherwise enamoured of English ways, who were often more English than the English.

17. Donaldson, op. cit., p. 203.

18. Ibid., p. 207.

III

THE MATTER OF WALES

Wales is the country within these islands where the problems of national identity are most acute and where the struggle to preserve it has had to be the most intense. Scotland may be able to take care of herself and Ireland is an island, but Wales is small and has no well-defined border between herself and England, and access to her most populous parts is easier from England than from other parts of Wales. Administratively, with only a few minor qualifications, she is part of England. This makes her language all the more precious as a badge of identity, but that language is in constant danger of being swamped by the all-pervasive dominance of English. It is no wonder that many Welshmen today feel that they live in a beleaguered city and that any concession to the enemy, especially when he comes bearing gifts, will mean that they will be completely overwhelmed and that all will be lost.

Without denying the reality of the problem, or the need for a strong re-affirmation of Welsh identity at the present time, this is not necessarily the most useful perspective in which to look at the matter of Wales. For looked at in another light, what is remarkable about Wales is the tenacity with which it has held to its national identity, from Roman times right up to the present day. Welshmen are proud of their history. Surely it is faint-heartedness to suppose that the forces which are abroad in the world today can do what Edward I and Henry VIII and the Anglicization of the gentry and the attempted suppression of the language and the industrial depression of the 1920s, perhaps the most serious blow to Wales of all, failed to do? The evidence suggests that, in the teeth of English television, the motor car, the Severn Bridge, the tourist industry, the flooding of Welsh valleys with water for England and of Welsh colleges with English students, the Welsh consciousness of national identity is as vigorous as ever, and a good deal more militant than hitherto.

This is not said in any spirit of complacency, as more fervently nationalistic Welshmen than myself might be disposed to allege, but in order to try to see the matter of Wales in the context of that of Britain as a whole and to ensure that Wales, as her distinctive self, makes her full contribution to the life of Britain. All nations have problems in maintaining their identity and a very small nation, which is politically part of a much larger unit, the majority of whose inhabitants are indifferent to it and ignorant about it, has acute problems. Yet the rule holds for small nations as for large. The price of continual survival in changing circumstances is adaptability. The English have learnt this so well in the course of their long history that they make their adaptations instinctively, so that they are carried out almost, if not quite, painlessly. The trouble with the English, indeed, is that their attitudes, and their institutions, have become so adaptable that it is now questionable whether some of them have any coherence at all. When they are confronted by the Welsh, they naturally assume that, with a little adaptation, their attitudes will serve very well for the Welsh also. They are genuinely puzzled as to why so many of the Welsh do not see things in this way. The Welsh see, even if the English do not, that they are a different people from the English and that, if they were doing things in their own way, they would have different attitudes and different institutions. Yet the very easy-going adaptability of the English makes it difficult for Welshmen to articulate what they might mean by these. Any concrete and workable suggestion that they make stands a good chance of being accepted, and yet accepted in such a way as to leave many Welshmen feeling vaguely frustrated, since they know that it will be set within a predominantly English framework.[1] Their reaction, therefore, often becomes a merely defensive one. They retreat into a world of their own, where they understand each other and where it is difficult for an interloper, however well-intentioned, to penetrate. They cease to be adaptable, and change itself comes to be regarded as an evil, something always engineered either by the English or by the Anglicized, who are no better than the English.

This attitude inevitably finds very clear expression in Welsh religious institutions, partly because nostalgia and conservative feelings always gather round a strong religious heritage but also because it was through their religion that the Welsh people recovered their own souls in the eighteenth and nineteenth centuries. It was supremely through the life of their own dissenting chapels, built by their own hands, that they found a road to personal maturity and independence which owed little or nothing to the English establishment and which often aroused its hostility. The chapels were their own, and once they were inside them no outside power could interfere with them. They were the shrines of their communal identity in the most intimately personal sense.

This has had some very interesting, and little noted,consequences. Probably in no Christian nation is the link closer than it has been in Wales between ordinary people and their church institutions. The nearest analogy may be found among some of the smaller sects in the USA, but there it is not linked so closely with the sense of national identity. As we have seen, the link of the Kirk with the nation is close in Scotland, but the power of the wider institutions, which have a measure of detachment from local and family life, is greater than it is in Wales, and the same is true of Irish Catholicism. It is to his own particular congregation and the people who make it up that the Welshman has his special bond of loyalty. The innumerable chapels which are such a feature of the Welsh landscape are a constant source of bewilderment to the English visitor. If he reflects upon them at all, he must wonder who built them and where the people come from who support them. If he tries to find out, he will not find the answer easily available. They are almost invariably shut up tight during the week and only occasionally are the times of services publicly announced. This happens not through any conscious desire to be secretive but because the members assume that everyone likely to be interested will know when things are happening or can easily find out through the informal contacts they have in the ordinary way of business. Surprise, generally pleasurable but occasionally slightly suspicious, is expressed when any outsider shows an interest. The chapels have come to think of themselves as virtually private affairs, more like families or at most clubs than public institutions open to all.[2]

This private, domestic character of chapel life is reflected in nearly all its activities, and produces some curious paradoxes. Welsh ministers are as interested as any others in civic, national and international affairs and frequently deal with them in sermons and discussions. The proportion of chapel members involved in community affairs is high. Most Welsh political leaders, especially in local government, still have a strong chapel connection, although it is probably not as strong as it was.[3] Yet it is not common for the members of the chapel as a group to do much in relation to wider community activity, except sometimes, often at Nationalist instigation, over a matter directly affecting Welsh identity. They have been involved in politics in the past, spectacularly over disestablishment of the Church in Wales and less spectacularly in relation to the depression and the anti-war movements, but nowadays as institutions they appear to find something alien in such involvement, except over the issue of national identity.

Similarly, Welsh-speaking chapels appear to have practically no policy on church extension, nor have they had for many years. It is true that the chief reasons for this are severely practical. There was extravagant over-building of chapels in the nineteenth century, when labour was cheap and materials were easily available. Population has been declining in the most intensely Welsh-speaking areas and familiarity with the Welsh language, until very recently, has been diminishing. All the same, there have been many movements of population, and there have been some limited but real opportunities for the relocating of churches and for the building of new ones, yet very few of them have been taken. The attitude seems to be exactly that of a family which has known better days. If the members are getting older and some of them are dying off, this is a natural fact about which nothing can be done. There is no point in trying to replenish the community with outsiders, since they do not belong, not sharing the family traditions nor being accustomed to its ways. When the children leave home, they can hardly be expected to link up with another church, unless they are lucky enough to find one near at hand which is just like the one they have left behind and which is part of the network of kinship, as they are able to in many districts of London.[4] Yet it would be regarded as a sign of disloyalty, of alienation from their identity, if they failed to take their place and be duly recognized in the local chapel on their visits home. This is why so many chapels in Wales give the impression of living in remarkably contented and peaceful retirement, while the attitude of many young people towards them is no longer that of the rebellious and critical young towards their parents, but that of indulgent, if strictly occasional, affection towards their grandparents.

This attitude is, perhaps, still the most characteristic among the Welsh people, but it does not tell the whole story about Welsh religious life nor about the Welsh national consciousness. Apart from anything else, the large majority of people who live in Wales are English-speaking. Of those who attend church services, the majority go to churches where the services are in English, although it is probably still true that, proportionately, Welsh speakers attend more than English speakers. The largest single group who attend English-speaking services do so in the Church of England in Wales, where the form of service and general atmosphere is much more like that which obtains in England than in Wales. Many of them, especially along the North Wales coast and in the larger towns of the South are, of course, themselves English.

Yet, after allowing for the presence of these English people, it would be quite wrong to assume that the cultural styles and loyalties of English-speaking Welsh people, whether in churches or outside them, are identical with those of their English neighbours. The majority, in fact the large majority, of those who live in the most thickly populated parts of Wales, particularly the coastal towns and industrial valleys of eastern South Wales, are monoglot English speakers, but in accent, style of living and sense of regional and national loyalty are much more akin to their Welsh-speaking brothers and sisters than to their English cousins. Whatever

Welsh nationalists may think about it, no outside observer is in much doubt that Dylan Thomas' Swansea is a different place from anywhere in England. One can sympathize with those Welsh-speaking Welshmen who protest that this is a sentimentalized caricature of what authentic Welshness is, and that it is tiresome when outsiders with some pretentions to sensitivity identify it with the real thing, but it underlines the fact that there is a very vigorous Anglo-Welsh society, which may not be fully Welsh according to their ideal of Welshness but which is emphatically not purely English either, and which shows little sign of being simply a transition stage to Englishness. Only those Welshmen who quite improperly identify Englishness with all that they most dislike in the internationalized popular culture of the modern world and who see the influence of this very strongly at work in places like Cardiff, Swansea and the industrialized valleys, could think otherwise.

The presence of this large Anglo-Welsh section of the community in Wales throws into relief one of the most difficult questions confronting Welshmen concerned for their identity today. How far is Wales really a separate nation? That it is, in very important respects, different from England and the rest of Britain, is not in dispute, but can it be realistically thought of as a separate nation? Is it no more than a semi-nation or a sub-nation within a larger unity, with many distinctive facets to its life but also with much in common with the other semi- or sub-nations of these islands? In the eyes of many Nationalists, even to raise this question is to lay rude hands on the ark of the Covenant. That Wales is self-evidently a separate nation is the basis of all Nationalist claims. Whatever answer may be given to this question, however, it must be firmly insisted against them that it is a perfectly proper, and indeed necessary, question to raise, especially if one maintains a Christian position. As we have seen, a Christian is committed to recognizing the relativity of all national loyalties. If, as we argue with some fierceness, the English have to face this kind of question, the Welsh can claim no exemption from it. Again, it is always the temptation of a small nation to assume that its smallness provides an excuse for avoiding the temptations which confront all forms of nationalism but, as with the young lady in the story, the fact that it is only a little baby is neither here nor there. Nor need any mature people feel that national honour demands that only the kind of answer which a fervent nationalist would want to give could be satisfactory. On the contrary, if it could be shown that Welsh people were able to retain a distinctive life of their own on some levels while they were able also to participate freely and as equals in the activities of a wider community and acknowledge a loyalty to it, this would be the greatest possible tribute to their maturity and civility. This, surely, is what everybody has to learn to be able to do if we are to survive without blowing each other up in the modern world.

The Welsh are, in fact, able to do this extremely well. They may not be able to do it as easily and effortlessly as the Scots, but the Welsh way of life is more distinctive and more closely-knit and less like that of the English than that of the Scots. They are still able to do it well, although it is doubtful whether they are able to do it as well in church life as in other spheres. Yet no one who does not believe it already is likely to be very convinced, especially in the present temper of Welsh-speaking Welsh life, unless an attempt is made to do justice to the Nationalist case. This is put forward with deep conviction, and it is one which commands the assent of many moderate and responsible people as well as of the small number of extremists whose activities inevitably attract English attention. As far as a relative outsider is able to understand the argument (while it is expressed clearly enough, it has to be recognized that someone who does not live all the time in Wales and is not involved in the nationalistic issue may well miss some of the overtones), it is that Wales will not be able properly to define, let alone express, her true identity unless she has political independence. Whether this independence should be complete in all respects, for example in relation to defence and foreign policy, is a matter of debate among Nationalists themselves, but there is substantial agreement among them that Wales needs her own parliament, the right to manage her own economy and educational system and the power to determine what cultural institutions and media of communication, like television, should receive public support. The Welsh language in particular, with all its intimate associations with Welsh history and tradition, expresses the Welsh spirit as nothing else does. Throw the language away and little that is distinctively Welsh will be left. Wales must have freedom to protect and foster the language, and concessions, often grudgingly granted, from English-dominated institutions are insufficient for the purpose. Throughout modern history Wales has been oppressed, if not entirely overwhelmed, by the sheer weight and size of England, even at times when she has not had to deal with English hostility. In all kinds of ways, obvious and subtle, Wales has been made to fit in with English convenience, so that it is hardly surprising that Welshmen no longer feel that they can call their souls their own. Many Nationalists would also hold that there is a special quality in Welsh life, democratic, personal, lyrical, free from commercial ambition and lust for power, which is not characteristic of the larger society, and that this is in danger of being crushed by the demands of that larger society. The latent Welshness of the many people in Wales who are Welsh but do not feel very strongly about it will only find expression when it becomes to their advantage to do so, when to be Welsh is to be part of the Establishment. Up to now, it has always been to people's advantage to become Anglicized. If Wales is to survive as a nation, this has to be changed.

Now it is essential to realize that there are many Welshmen, whose credentials to be Welsh spokesmen could not be challenged even by the straitest sect of the Nationalists, who do not accept the arguments just outlined, or at least not without substantial qualification. They believe that for Wales political independence is as unreal as that economic independence for which Nationalist economists argue. Apart from any other considerations, and there are plenty of those, they are sure that the vast majority of residents do not want it and do not show the slightest signs of being prepared to pay the price which it would demand. These are the inhabitants of the most populous parts of Wales and the parts which are growing most rapidly. Any realistic strategy for the fostering of Welsh identity, they would argue, must give up trying to make large and futile gestures which give those who make them the comforting illusion that they are putting up a great fight but which can win no more than a few small gains at the price of creating a good deal of ill-feeling among people who ought to be working together. Concern for the preservation of Welsh identity is the preoccupation of a minority, and a diminishing minority at that, diminishing in statistical terms if not in terms of quality.[5] Intelligent Welshmen should operate like all well-informed minorities who hope to influence majorities, by making practical and reasonable demands which win friends and influence people, and doing so by the quiet but permanently effective ways of democratic persuasion. 'Direct action' tactics by 'militants' may well earn short-term results, in the way a noisy child may get something to stop him hollering, but they owe more to the current international fashion for spectacular protest than to anything distinctive in the Welsh genius, and they lose the respect, and sometimes the affection, which Welsh people have built up over the years among the more perceptive of their neighbours, and poison the atmosphere for the creation of the more important and more durable expansion of the area of Welsh identity.

The fact that many Welshmen, including, let it be said, many members of Plaid Cymru, the Welsh Nationalist Party, think this should not, however, lead English people to do what they are always only too eager to do, to use it as an excuse for discounting the revival of Welsh self-consciousness as being the work of a few eccentric extremists. Even if only a minority of Welshmen are Nationalists, that minority contains many of the liveliest and ablest members of the nation. Their opinions, and the opinions of many who sympathize, without necessarily fully agreeing, with them are worthy of the respectful attention of anyone concerned for the health of the common life of these islands. And, as the Kilbrandon report clearly recognizes, the majority of thoughtful Welshmen share the concern of the Nationalists for re-emphasizing national identity and would support some, if not all, of their aims. Even if it is both more mixed and pervasive, as well as tougher, than most Nationalists believe, there is a Welsh identity, and most Welshmen believe that it is worth going to a good deal of trouble to cherish it. The Welsh heartland in Gwynedd, Dyfed and Powys, which is Welsh-speaking and does most to nourish that

identity, is shrinking and deserves help. This is far more true of
Wales than it is of Scotland, except for Gaelic Scotland, whose
plight is more desperate even than that of Wales. Wales needs help
but, if the help is to be well-directed, Wales needs to be understood, and Wales cannot be understood if those outside her
community who are in a position to help refuse to take her distinct
identity seriously. English people must realize that the Welsh have
suffered more damage to their sense of identity than any other
nation and, for some of them, the difficulties they experience in
dealing with the English are beginning to create neuroses. These
may not yet be very many, but any Englishman who is concerned
for the unity and harmony and well-being of all the inhabitants of
these islands will see this as a danger-signal and begin to pay more
careful attention to the Welsh.

For Wales to succumb to this sickness would be devastating. At
the end of his remarkable epic novel, *Owen Glendower*, John
Cowper Powys makes his hero, who is in hiding and at the point of
death, say this,

> Why shouldn't the whole race of Wales increase its power by sinking
> inwards, rather than by winning external victories . . . why shouldn't she
> be the one single race—along with the Jews of course!—who win by
> losing?[6]

It is a dangerously tempting prospect for a reflective Celtic race
with a long memory and faced with daunting frustrations. The
trouble is that it will not work, and it is good that it will not work.
Christian people, and most Welsh people still claim to be Christian,
should have none of it because it is moved by resentment, self-pity
and hate, and it is the opposite of that dying to live of which the
real faith of the New Testament speaks. It is not an accident that
the God whom Owen goes on to invoke in this passage, deliberately misreading a poem of Taliessin in doing so, is not the
Christian God, who is the Father of us all, but an ancient pre-
Christian Brythonic God. For Wales to follow this road is to deny
all that is living and healthy in the tradition of modern Wales,
because Welsh identity has always been at its strongest when
Welsh Christian faith has been at its deepest.

Like all peoples, but again perhaps more than most, the Welsh are at their best when they are not turned in upon themselves and brooding on their failures, like the defeated Owen Glendower in the novel, but when their natural warmth and expansiveness have a chance to express themselves in a generous impulse. Nowhere were evacuees received with more open-heartedness than in the Welsh valleys during the war, and there is a unique quality of delight about the welcome given to the Fiji rugby players in Wales which no other part of these islands can begin to emulate. There are more elegant and more efficient large towns in Britain than Swansea, but none where the casual visitor is more aware of being in a community of friendly and sympathetic people who are unaffectedly interested in him as a human being. It must be remembered, however, that their history and their social circumstances, which have often in the past involved a good deal of economic hardship, have prevented many of the Welsh from having that self-contained independence of the Lowland Scot in moving out into a wider world. They are more 'other-directed', and they need the encouragement of a warm welcome if the best that is in them is to become manifest. This is particularly true when they meet their rich and powerful English neighbours. But to be warmly welcoming is not a characteristic English virtue, and the English need to have this in mind in dealing with the Welsh. This becomes more, and not less, important to the extent that it is impracticable for Wales to go her own way because we are so inextricably bound up with each other in the life of these islands. Good manners as well as good sense demand that every respect be paid by her close neighbours to what is distinctive in her life.

There is one matter, in particular, to which English people should pay far more attention, and far more intelligent attention, than they normally do. It is precisely that of the Welsh language. The ignorance of many quite educated English people on this matter is inexcusable and does something, although perhaps not much, to justify the antics of the Welsh Language Society. The Welsh language is one of the great cultural treasures of these islands, and no educated Englishman can claim to be familiar with the British tradition unless he is aware of the fact. It is not in any sense an archaic language, kept alive in the limited circle of a folk culture. It is a classical language comparable to the great languages of the European tradition, magnificently evocative, capable of being disciplined into the richest of poetic forms, a fitting vehicle for the expression of the profoundest insight and yet robust enough for everyday use in the rapidly changing modern world. Nothing would be a clearer proof of new seriousness on the part of the English towards the Welsh than that an introduction to Welsh language and literature should become part of the curriculum of English schools, and English schools in England are meant here, as a necessary part of understanding and appreciation of the best of our common British cultural heritage.[7]

It is this kind of action on the part of the English which might begin to convince the Welsh that English people really treat them as distinctive members of the British community in their own right and not as slightly funny second-class Englishmen. This, in its turn, might help some Welshmen to take the chips off their shoulders and check the growth of that most uncharacteristic intolerant exclusiveness which seems to be spreading in some Welsh circles today. When, for example, Mr Ned Thomas, in his book *The Welsh Extremists*, tries to commend the Nationalist case to English readers, he does so by giving a heavily nostalgic and idealized account of Welsh life, but finds little to admire in England except a few fashionable writers who have little affinity with the Welsh spirit but are united in their dislike of most aspects of life in their own country. As he himself rightly says:

As English population floods in to Wales, we shall need more and more to provide a culture that not so much defends itself by exclusion, as absorbs people by its superior humanity.[8]

Wales can do this but, before she does so, it might be wise to ask what the automatic use of the word 'superior' in that context reveals about the attitude of some of her modern children.

The truth is that the great majority of Welsh people, whether they be primarily Welsh- or English-speaking, are quite clear on these two points. First, they are Welsh and not English and want to remain so. The attitude of many of them to the language is rather like the attitude of equally many of them to their chapels. They are glad that they are there and recognize some degree of obligation and loyalty to them, even though they do precious little to ensure their continued existence. Because of this, both chapel and language have a point of contact on which to build if they do not try to rush people into commitments which they are not yet ready to make. But, despite their ambivalence on these important matters, to be Welsh means something quite definite to them—an accent, a rich body of folk memories, a warm and unpretentious and very democratic style of life, their soft green hills and valleys, their hymns and songs of spontaneous eloquence—and they love it and want to keep it. Secondly, they want to participate on equal terms with everyone else in the life of Britain and in that of the modern world in general. They resent any effort, whether by Nationalists or by anyone else, to prevent them doing this. This is true on every level, whether that of the life of international high culture, of the ordinary life of Britain or of the 'pop-scene'. They are Welsh and proud of it and they are British too, and also proud of it, and they see no earthly reason and no heavenly one either, why they should not be both.[9] Given Wales' situation, it is not enough only to be Welsh. You have to share in a wider community. To pretend otherwise is mere wilfulness or escapism. There is such a wider community in which the Welsh share, one with which they are inextricably involved every day, that of the British nation. Most Welshmen would agree that Welsh identity needs to be more sharply stated in the British context today, but they take it for granted, as a self-evident truth, that that context is inevitable and must remain.

The statement that there was no heavenly reason for Welsh isolationism was, of course, deliberately made. What it meant was that the Welsh Christian commitment points in the other direction, that of strengthening the ties between Wales and her neighbours and, in particular, rooting out the resentment of the English which beats in many Welsh hearts. Those Welsh Christians who feel called to give their best energies to the reassertion of Welsh identity owe it to their fellow-Christians to define what it is in the Welsh outlook and way of life which is so precious that it must be preserved at all costs. What theological insights, liturgical practices and forms of social witness do their churches have which English and other churches would reject and which they believe must be maintained? What generous and positively Christian causes do Welsh churches espouse which run counter to the will of the rest of Christendom?[10] It is not implied that they do not exist, only that they have not been explained, but perhaps it is implied that, when they are explained, many people in England and in other lands would say that they are in favour of them and would like to co-operate with Welsh people in relation to them. If Welsh people were to reply, as many of them might, that the English, and through the English, the international Christian world, was so large and so dominating that their own particular approach even on matters of common concern was overlooked, and that they needed to go their own way for a time to find their own soul again, even in Christian terms, this is an attitude which sensitive outsiders should be able to appreciate and respect. But it provides no excuse for the defensiveness, and occasional hostility, which are often displayed. Welshmen need to have confidence in their own religious traditions, as in their language, and to believe that it is possible for those who are not Welsh, or are only partly Welsh, to come and admire them and share in them as far as they are able. The Welsh will find their true identity not in isolation from but in dialogue with their neighbours. For that dialogue to be effective, they may need to make some temporary withdrawals so as to stand sufficiently apart from their neighbours to make conversation possible and their neighbours, particularly the English, will have to make a much greater effort than they have ever done in the past really to listen to what Wales has to say in Wales' own terms. But Wales must make an effort to say it, and Christian Wales should know how to say it in a Christian way.

NOTES

1. P. J. Madgwick, op. cit., p. 243, mentions the Welsh Nationalist who complains of the difficulty of finding tangible grievances to exploit and of the dangers of cultural assimilation: that non-Welsh people might by their sympathy 'suffocate the Welshness of Welsh institutions'.

2. This attitude is so deep-rooted that it extends itself even into situations where it cannot possibly be considered appropriate. Thus, Jewin Presbyterian Church, a large, old-established and influential Welsh-speaking congregation on the edge of the City of London, which draws its people from a wide area, was rebuilt on spacious lines after being bombed during the war but, until a handsome notice in appropriate Welsh slate finally appeared in 1974, revealed no clues whatsoever to the passer-by as to its identity except for a small foundation stone which says nothing about the nature of the institution or the times of its activities but does inform the world in impeccable Welsh that this stone was laid by the Lord Mayor of London in 1966.

3. See T. Brennan, E. H. Cooney and E. Pollin, *Social Change in South-West Wales*, Watts 1954, and Madgwick, op. cit.; also Elwyn Davies and Alwyn D. Rees (eds.), *Welsh Rural Communities*, University of Wales Press 1960, especially the articles on Aberporth by David Jenkins and on Glanllyn by Trefor M. Owen.

4. As David Martin puts it in suitably sociological language, their religion 'has acquired a degree of particularity in relation to the local structures of kin which is very easily corroded by extensive and continuous geographical mobility', *A Sociology of English Religion*, SCM Press 1967, p. 93.

5. In so far as ability to speak the language is a guide to concern for Welsh identity, 20·6% of the population were able to speak it in 1971 compared with 26% in 1961, although there were some signs of revival, especially among children and young people.

6. John Cowper Powys, *Owen Glendower*, John Lane 1941, p. 914.

7. A beginning could easily be made here by the Schools programme of the BBC.

8. Ned Thomas, *The Welsh Extremists*, Gollancz 1971, p. 121.

9. This is brought out very clearly at many points in Madgwick's study of political life in Cardiganshire, one of the most quintessentially Welsh of counties.

10. It is disappointing that no attempt is made to answer these questions by a theologian well-equipped to do so, in a recent apologia for Welsh Nationalism written for English readers: R. Tudur Jones, *The Desire of Nations*, Christopher Davies, Llandybie 1974.

IV

THE ENGLISH AND THEIR CHURCHES

1   *England and Britain*

The crux of the matter of Britain lies in making English people see that there is a matter of Britain which is different from the matter of England. To the typical Englishman, Britain is England. He is puzzled when someone points out that the Union Jack is not the English flag and that it is insulting for English supporters to wave it when England play games against Scotland or Wales. Of course, he knows that Scotland, Wales and the rest exist, but for him they do so only as touches of colour on the fringes of British life, which receives its style and stamp from the all-determining influence of England. Americans have long been familiar with the old Bostonian map of the United States, which gives an enormous area to the neighbourhood of Boston, recorded in loving detail, a modest space to the rest of New England and New York, and vague nonentity to the great land-mass beyond. Fortunately, our smaller size and system of parliamentary representation makes people who live in London more aware of the country as a whole than that, but the relative importance given to various parts of these islands in determining national attitudes by the London-based English is not dissimilar.

The reasons for this lie deeper than in those of ordinary metropolitan self-centredness, for they pervade the whole life of the nation. Throughout all their long history, the English have had few occasions on which they have been forced to be introspective or even to make comparisons between themselves and other peoples on the basis of equality. Their island situation, where they have not been the sole, but have nearly always been the overwhelmingly dominant nation, has obviously greatly helped in this. No other major nation can rival the length of unbroken institutional continuity that England has enjoyed, nor the freedom from foreign occupation or domination. When self-questioning has proved inescapable, as it did in the seventeenth century and the early Victorian era, it proved just sufficient, with only one brief gap, to make the adjustments necessary to meet far-reaching changes without radical breaks in continuity. Neither the Glorious Revolution of 1688 nor the Industrial Revolution were really revolutionary as far as English life was concerned. It was the most self-confident and least self-critical elements in the nation's leadership who emerged victorious from both crises.

Even the special kind of island situation which England has enjoyed has worked to her advantage, in that the British Isles are large enough to allow plenty of internal movement and accessible enough from outside to provide plenty of international communication. Few English people have ever experienced claustrophobia because of their insularity. It is only American visitors who have felt in danger of falling off the island. Over many generations also, large numbers of her most vigorous children have been able to find an outlet for their energies in overseas trade, military adventure, colonial expansion and missionary service, yet all in such a way as to enrich rather than impoverish her domestic life, since England remained large, metropolitan and attractive enough always to remain as 'home'. The fact that many of the same opportunities have also been available to the Welsh and the Scots, although generally under less favourable conditions and in ways which often did serve to impoverish their homelands, has meant that they have been able to find an outlet for any frustrations they might experience about their subordinate situation by going abroad or by trying to make their fortune in England itself. The result has been that the possibilities of any serious internal international confrontation have been steadily diminishing, at least until very recently, ever since the last abortive attempt at one was made in 1745.

The strength, resilience and tenacity of the society built up so steadily and continuously over the centuries is one of the wonders of the world. Its very lack of self-consciousness is a sign of how deep the roots of its assurance about itself are. The favourite English image of itself as being like a great and ancient oak is not an inappropriate one. England has been at the centre of world events for several centuries and has had to endure many storms. She has withstood them so firmly that there has hardly ever been a time when she has been conscious of any tearing at her roots. Even though she had experienced the terrible blood-letting of the First World War and the enervating years of the depression in what was almost the same generation, the threat to her existence in 1940 did not shake her but rather filled her with new confidence in herself. She has also managed to build up a great empire and, almost immediately, to surrender its control to others without losing the goodwill of most of her former subjects or going sour upon herself, an achievement without parallel in history. To be top nation is never an attractive role in the eyes of those who do not share your good fortune. The English have probably been able to fulfil it with as much grace as any nation ever has, and not the least graceful thing about it has been the way in which they have relinquished that role to others.

Yet while this unself-conscious assurance and ability to maintain continuity has been a great source of strength to England in her period of dominance and has helped her to 'hang on' and to 'muddle through' in times of crisis, it may not be so helpful in the very confusing situation in which she finds herself today. For it is a situation in which she has to walk warily if she is to avoid unnecessary trouble and to be quick in perception if she is to see and to seize new opportunites to strengthen her internal life and extend her international influence. Those English people who have a proprietorial stake in the country, the 'top people' and also, in this matter, a large number of those among them who also pride themselves on having 'lively minds', still find it hard to accept the notion that they are only one nation among the peoples of the world, subject to the same laws as those which influence the evolution of all societies. It is only of slight consolation to be able to recognize that their fathers would have found it harder and their grandfathers even harder yet. Many of the greatest dangers to a nation, as to a church, arise as a consequence of its success, and the very achievement of the English in providing such a strong sense of national identity and in maintaining institutional continuity for so long has led them to possess not merely that conviction of their own uniqueness which all nations have but also a belief that their most characteristic institutions are not so much functional structures, like any other organization, as permanent elements in the inalienably given order of the universe. The monarchy, the ancient universities and the public schools, the British navy and, nowadays to a lesser degree, the Church of England and *The Times*, are part of the very substance of Englishness and one might as well question their necessity as one would that of the English weather and the English country landscape. One is free to grumble about them, but only on the ground that they are not being true to themselves. To call their basis into question is to cast doubts on one's own authenticity as an Englishman.

All the same, a new period of self-questioning seems to be forcing itself upon the reluctant English today, and they must learn to submit themselves to it if they are to survive. Otherwise the ravages of mobility, technologically-induced triviality and the erosion of the cultural soil created by excessively large cities in England's inner life, and radical changes in her international position, combined with the new assertiveness of the Scots and the Welsh, may all combine to do in this century what two world wars have failed to do. It is important that she should submit to this self-questioning, and the possibility of self-criticism which it brings, with a good grace, and for these three reasons.

First, English self-confidence can only have arisen among those who have enjoyed power and privilege. Power and privilege can never be taken for granted because their exercise always involves a measure of exploitation of others. The rulers of the English have come to see this, not easily of course, but not unimpressively either as history goes, in their dealings with former colonial peoples. The very disparity between their position and that of their former dependents has helped them to acknowledge this and to do something about it. They have always found it harder to see it in their dealings with the Scots and the Welsh, just as many of them still find it hard to see it in their dealings even with those fellow-Englishmen who do not share the same set of institutional loyalties as they do. Their assumption is that others should be content with the role of poor relation because they are, after all, recognized as members of the family. But if the Scots and Welsh say they are discriminated against, as many of them do, it is not enough for the dominant partner in the relationship to say that he cannot see what the fuss is about. Whether he likes it or not, he has to try to find out, to see whether there is anything wrong that needs to be put right. It would be a pity to have to wait until they make such nuisances of themselves as the people of Northern Ireland have before he can be driven to take much interest in their complaints.

Secondly, this attitude ignores present power realities. The English are still a considerable nation, but they are no longer 'top people' among the nations, nor are the top people among the English themselves as much on top as they were. The only sensible thing to do in such a situation is to face the facts and make the necessary adjustments. Harsh realities compel us to do this fairly quickly in economic and military affairs, where power realities are easily quantifiable. In more imponderable matters of attitude and style, we can cherish illusions longer. For example, it is only now that the myth is dissolving that although the Americans are richer than we are, they are also less cultured. 'A tranquil consciousness of effortless superiority' becomes undignified and, indeed, ridiculous when you are in fact struggling to keep in touch at all with the leaders in the race. There is some dignity in the sensible acceptance of changed circumstances. There is none in the pretence of power and influence without the reality. Exiled noblemen who are always clutching about them the trappings of their former state in the hope of exacting deference from new neighbours who owe them nothing, succeed only in raising questions as to whether their fall from glory was not deserved.

Thirdly, this attitude breeds complacency, and complacency is always corrosive and could ultimately be destructive. The fact that the heritage of England is, in so many ways, a good one and well worthy of being preserved and enjoyed, makes this more and not less true.. It is one of the hardest lessons of experience that you cannot continue to enjoy the best of your heritage if all you are content to do is simply to enjoy it. The warnings of the experience of the old Israel apply to England just as much as to any other country. The conditions of being genuinely creative are the same for all people. If the past is to be handed on in a fresh and living way and new things are to emerge, there must be venture and risk, just as much for English empiricists as for continental existentialists. England has to learn reflective self-criticism about the very roots of her national existence if, in the world we know today, she is to have a future and if she is to preserve for her future the best of her past.

2   The Church of England

It is one of the main public functions of a church which receives widespread popular support in a nation, and especially of a church which is prepared to accept the position of being part of the state establishment, to call the attention of that nation to the need for this self-criticism. It is what repentance means on the level of national identity, *metanoia*, turning away from self-preoccupation to the rediscovery of God's will, which always involves the rejection of some aspects of one's past and a resolution to make a fresh start. This is why, for Christian people, the position of the Church of England is crucial for understanding the matter of England.

Any Protestant Dissenter who lives in England and tries to write about the Church of England must be conscious of the ease with which his judgment can be distorted because of the prejudices he himself is likely to have acquired. In this instance, at least, there may be some countervailing consideration in the fact that the judgment is based on a warm and positive appreciation of the role which the Church of England has played as an established church in the course of English history. It is in this context only that the assertion is made that it has always been more characteristic of the Church of England to express the national attitude described in the preceding section than to set a question mark against it. More than that, its representatives have sometimes expressed it even more clearly than those of other institutions, partly because, in contrast to the monarchy and Parliament and most of the other institutions already mentioned, it is the most exclusively English of all our major institutions. This is true despite the existence of the world-wide Anglican communion. The obituary notice of Archbishop Randall Davidson in one of the national newspapers said that 'he gave perfect expression to public sentiments on national occasions'. This was obviously intended to be complimentary, an appropriate exercise of his office as the first subject of the monarch, and there can be little doubt that the majority of Anglican Englishmen, both clerical and lay, would have regarded it as such. One wonders what an Anglican Kierkegaard, if such a phenomenon can have any degree of credibility, might have made of such a statement.

To start off in this way is not to imply that this is the whole truth about the relation of the Church of England to the English nation, or even the most important part of the truth. On the contrary, the further one goes into this question, the more possible it becomes to take a more favourable view of the Church of England as an established church than many Anglicans themselves seem prepared to take at present. This is quite apart from the fact that there are, of course, many other aspects to the Church of England than that of establishment, and aspects of great importance to Christianity and to British common life. Anglicanism in its occasional moods of narcissistic self-love rouses its critics, internal as well as external, to fury. But when Anglicanism is looked at as one Christian denomination among others, and especially as one among the established churches of the world, its virtues as well as its defects begin to shine forth more clearly. After all, it stands to reason that any institution which has held the allegiance of the best in the dominant groups in its own highly successful community over many centuries and through many vicissitudes is bound to possess great qualities. The cathedrals and parish churches of England are among England's greatest glories, not merely as architectural monuments but as buildings lovingly cherished and in daily use, and they stand out as such today as much as, if not more than, they ever did.

Dietrich Bonhoeffer, the German theologian executed by the Nazis, was one of the first theologians in modern times to look at some of the issues raised by the church's success in the world,[1] but much more thought needs to be given to them in these days. It is a sign of spiritual sickness, of defeatism, which is an indication of secret unbelief, when the first reaction to any kind of success in the world is to assume that it can only have happened because people have had wrong Christian priorities. One wonders whether modern Christian prophets of 'secularization', who are often to be found within the Church of England herself, have thought out the implications of what they say they want. They argue, and up to a point quite rightly, for the identification of the church, by which they too often mean the church's professional ministers, with the secular concerns of men, as they go about their business in this world. No church has identified itself more completely with the life of those who shaped the destinies of their own communities than the Church of England has throughout its history. Whatever ambiguities may attach to the English Reformation, there is no denying that a large part of its impetus derived from the conviction of churchmen that their first duty lay with the lives of their own people rather than with following the dictates of a foreign power whose claim to represent the true community of the Church of Christ was seen to be increasingly unreal. That the Church of England, continuing in this spirit throughout the centuries which followed, succumbed to the temptations of the enterprise and failed sufficiently to distinguish between the will of God for England and the will of the ruling classes for England is a fact of which no Protestant Dissenter needs to be reminded. Some of her modern internal critics, however, while advocating 'secularization', seem to deplore the fact that she ever made the effort and are embarrassed by the success which has enabled her to maintain her position as the established church right to this day.

This frankly, is hard to understand. As someone brought up outside England, in a church not in communion with the Church of England, I am not prepared voluntarily to accept the burden of all the ambiguities and betrayals which the Church of England has to carry as part of her heritage, except as part of a widespread movement of reunion which involves radical changes for all parties concerned. From the outside, the price would be too high to pay. But those who have been brought up as Anglicans and are, therefore, placed in a situation where they have to take responsibility for this heritage, should surely take some encouragement in dealing with the massive problems which confront them from the thought that for a Christian community to reach the position of being an established church is itself a testimony to the power of grace. What is more, for a church to maintain itself in this obviously dangerous position for many long generations without becoming completely corrupted is a sign that grace has not been absent from her midst throughout her history. Even though that grace has come in a form no more dramatic than that of 'continual dew', to use the quaintly prophetic phrase of the Prayer Book, the quality of English life throughout the ages when it has been significantly touched by the church gives a good deal more than a hint that it has been present.

Thus when the worst has been said about the Church of England, and an attempt will shortly be made to say the worst, this church has managed to do what the Bible tells us, and experience confirms, is one of the most difficult things in history, to convert many of the rich and powerful to living Christian faith and then to go on to do what is even more difficult, to convert many of their children and their children's children after them. In her own life, her leaders, if not always the rank and file of her clergy, have often become rich and powerful. In the process they have inevitably shown some of the corruption of power, but rarely to such an extent that self-criticism and the possibility of renewal have been shut out of the church. If the Church of England cannot claim to demonstrate very vividly how to be born again when one is old, she has shown a remarkable capacity to ward off the most distressing signs of the onset of old age. Her more ruggedly masculine counterpart, the Church of Rome, tries to maintain the full vigour of maturity as long as possible lest, if any letting up is allowed, everything falls apart. *Ecclesia Anglicana* is more like a charming lady of uncertain age who is discreet and sensible enough to make the most of her autumn and prolong it as long as possible by not overdoing things. To act in this way may be less than the whole of what the Church of

God is meant to be in the world but, if a realistic view of the evolution of ecclesiastical institutions is taken, it is possible to be grateful that she still goes so quietly and sensibly about her business in a very imperfect world.

Nevertheless, the fact remains that, however sensible you may be in prolonging the days of autumn, winter will inevitably come and no spring will follow it unless you are prepared to take more radical action about yourself than the Church of England constitutionally, in more than one sense of the word, has ever been able to do. The Church of England today is very far indeed from being a dying church. There are many shoots of new life springing up among her old stones and, on some levels of her life, she is showing more reformist zeal than ever before in her history. For the most part, however, all this is not very different from what goes on in other major Christian denominations. What is significant from the point of view of the argument of this book is that the Church of England gives the impression that she has lost heart about her role as the church of the English people, possessing a deep and intimate connection with the English sense of national identity, and that she is resigning herself to conducting a retreat, characteristically slow and cautious, into denominational status.

This is deplorable. The objections to be made against the Church of England as an established church today from the point of view of our argument are almost the opposite of those traditionally made by Dissenters. These were that it was obsequiously servile to the ruling political powers, oppressive or snobbishly aloof to all outsiders and resentful of any sign of new religious vitality as dangerously 'enthusiastic' and disruptive of the prevailing order. But our objection is that while she still clings to the trappings of establishment, the Church of England is more interested in herself as an institution than she is in England and is failing to think imaginatively enough about the future of England in the light of the Christian faith. If England can no longer take her own identity for granted, the Church of England should take the lead in helping her to make a fresh and constructive self-examination. She is not only failing to do so. If the wan little report on relations between church and state brought out by an Archbishop's Commission in

1970 is any guide,[2] she no longer even sees the necessity of trying. This makes it hard to see what justification there ever was for her position as an established church.

The idea of 'the Establishment' is much spoken against in these days. Even beneficed clergy and residentiary canons of the Church of England have been heard to join in the chorus of denunciation, which prompts in the outsider the reflection that this is on a moral level comparable to that of joining a mob who are flinging mud at one's elderly mother in case they might realize that you are one of her children and turn in their wrath upon you. It is true that the word 'Establishment' is very loosely used in popular discussion, often being merely a term of abuse for those in positions of influence whom one dislikes in situations where it is difficult to pin responsibility for unpopular actions on anyone in particular. But in British life, it is perfectly possible to use the word precisely. It refers to those who hold permanent positions in essential public services, particularly the civil and armed services, the administration and enforcement of the law and, in her own way, the Church of England herself. Understood in this sense, it is the members of the Establishment who, above all other sections of the community, should be the special objects of the intellectual interest and pastoral concern of the Church of England 'as by law established'. Its leaders are conveniently located in a small area of Westminster. A large proportion of them, far more than in the population as a whole, are devoted Christians or are, at least, ready to be sympathetic. Some of them carry enormous responsibilities and many of them are hard pressed to find someone independent and trustworthy to whom they can talk about their personal and public problems. The Church of England would appear to be quite magnificently equipped to provide the help which they need. Not only should she possess the insight and fellow-feeling derived from being herself part of the Establishment but her physical resources are ideal for the purpose. Across the road from the Houses of Parliament stands the great Abbey of Westminster, which provides not only an incomparable setting for great religious occasions of state but also a number of attractive houses and apartments for hospitality and informal conversation. A few steps beyond are Dean's Yard and

Church House, with all the facilities they are able to provide. Across the river is Lambeth Palace and its park. But what use does the Church of England make of all this in order to fulfil this part of her responsibility as the Establishment? Some things are certainly done. Successive rectors of St Margaret's have done a great deal for Members of Parliament and, under the present enlightened leadership, the staff of the Abbey have an imaginative approach to their national responsibility to which there are few rivals. The Board of Social Responsibility of the Church of England, located in Church House, does excellent work for the church as a whole, although not always in direct association with Westminster and Whitehall, but it has no specific pastoral role. Without disparaging what is done, does it, however, begin to add up to what might be expected of the established church in relation to the rest of the Establishment, given the resources which are available and the intricate nature of the situation in which the English Establishment finds itself? If it be argued that work of this kind should, of course, be ecumenical in these days, we should agree, but still ask in that case why, for example, no chaplaincy facilities are provided for the established Church of Scotland or the non-established Free Churches of Wales within or near the Palace of Westminster. The main responsibility, and the power of initiative, rests with the church which still keeps all the privileges of establishment firmly in her own hands.

The Church of England shows a similar lack of will on the more general level of ideas. There has been a sad decline in the quality of Anglican thinking about England in the twentieth century as compared with the nineteenth, a decline which has gone along with a lack of enterprise and conviction in maintaining leadership within some of the institutions through which Anglican ideals for England have been traditionally expressed, like the public schools and the ancient universities. With one or two exceptions shortly to be mentioned, there has been nothing in this century to match the quality of thinking about the established church in relation to society of Coleridge and Thomas Arnold, of Maurice and Gladstone. There was a sense in which the Archbishop of Canterbury was the leader of the cultural life of England in the nineteenth century. In one of his autobiographical essays,[3] A. N. Whitehead speaks of the deep impression made upon him by the visit of Archbishop Tait to his father's Thanet rectory. Here was the leading representative of English culture sitting in their family drawing-room. The Church of England could make some show of meeting Coleridge's expectation that it could become a truly national church in this sense, and its clergy and educated laymen were able to display some of the character of his clerisy in an age when Gladstone could speak without affectation of the 'God-fearing and God-sustaining university of Oxford'. It would be hard to think in such terms today. The one twentieth-century archbishop who had the intellectual ability, range of interests and personal standing to qualify him for a position of national leadership comparable to that of some of his nineteenth-century predecessors was William Temple. It is worth remembering that, aided by the unification of the nation and the seriousness of temper which were engendered by the Second World War, he very nearly regained it. With the quiet help in the background of J. H. Oldham, a Christian clerisy not altogether incommensurate with the task before them was created in those years. But Temple's untimely death in 1944 set matters back and, with the coming of peace, it became increasingly clear that the heart of the Church of England was not in the enterprise.

It is a curious, and little noted, fact that many of the best statements of the social function of the Church of England came either from people who were not brought up as Anglicans or from those who were exposed to non-Anglican influences at significant periods in their lives. This was true even in the nineteenth century. Coleridge was a son of the rectory but he became a Unitarian at a formative stage in his development and had to look at Anglicanism from the outside before he became its apologist. F. D. Maurice, whose restatement of Anglicanism is probably the most attractive to twentieth-century minds, was brought up a Unitarian and Gladstone had a Scottish background and a Welsh home, while most of his political support came from Dissenters. Even the Tait who so impressed the young Whitehead was a Scot. Newman's *Idea of the University*, the classic exposition of the

Oxford ideal of education for the clerisy, although he did not use the term, was delivered as a series of lectures by a Roman convert to a bewildered Irish audience about founding a Roman Catholic university in their country. It is, if anything, even more true in the twentieth century. Between the wars, the most determined effort of our century to restate a distinctively Anglican view of society was made by a group who would probably have been prepared to describe themselves as representatives of Coleridge's clerisy, the Anglo-Catholic Christendom group already mentioned. Yet three of the most prominent members of this group, T. S. Eliot, V. A. Demant and Philip Mairet, were not brought up as Anglicans, and this was true of several others of them. Similarly, some of the most penetrating internal criticisms of Anglicanism were made in the *Essays in Anglican Self-Criticism* brought out under the editorship of David Paton in 1958.[4] Yet most of these essays were written by people who had either a strong non-Anglican element in their upbringing or who had been stimulated by missionary service overseas to look at Anglicanism in a fresh light. This suggests that it is very hard for the Church of England, left to herself, to engender the kind of self-awareness which prompts her members to do anything more than maintain the institution in traditional ways, making only those modifications which have so much of the 'inevitability of gradualness' as to be almost imperceptible while they are in process of happening. If this is true, it is important for understanding where the springs of vitality are to be found in British life. This may partly explain why the otherwise quite remarkable growth of world-wide Anglicanism has had so little effect on Anglican thinking about the role of the Church of England in English life. The Anglican communion is undoubtedly a reality. The Lambeth Conference is a major Anglican event and Archbishops of Canterbury take their role of primacy in the Anglican communion with great seriousness. Yet, for all the excellent study material generated by the Lambeth Conference, it has given little attention to the relation between Anglican churches and the various nations in which they find themselves, or to the peculiar Englishness of the Church of England and the problems which this raises for non-English Anglicanism.[5] This lack of interest in the problems raised by Englishness may be partly due to the fact that so many non-English Anglicans are passionately Anglophile and have been attracted to the Anglican communion for that reason. This may be a tribute to the charm of the Anglican style of life, but it does not help to frame realistic policies in relation to the peculiar national and international responsibilities of Anglican churches in their own situations, which are often radically different from that of England.[6]

The mischievous notion cannot be suppressed that, just as the British Empire was built in a fit of absent-mindedness, so was the Anglican communion, but that not a few English Anglicans consider it to have been a mistake, except where its overseas members have been content to make their churches carbon copies of the Church of England at home. This becomes very visible at pan-Anglican conferences, when some English bishops do not entirely succeed in concealing their dislike of their American colleagues for being rich, powerful and Anglican, and yet not English. The amount of resentment felt by many of their own clergy against the international activities of English bishops prominent in the ecumenical movement is as disconcerting as it is revealing. This was true even of such an outstanding Anglican and Englishman as Bishop Bell of Chichester, whom most ecumenical churchmen considered as representative of Anglicanism, and England, at their very best. The complaint was not that he neglected essential diocesan duties but that to be so interested in the rest of the world in that way was somehow non-Anglican. The idea was that a good Anglican should be content to stay at home and work within the system, relating any changes which might be needed to strictly local considerations. To be willing to speak as an Anglican among the churches and to be so actively concerned for the well-being of Christians in other lands was a subtle derogation of Anglicanism's precious uniqueness.

This sense of uniqueness bound up with a feeling of national identity, and its highly ambiguous relation to the Christian faith as understood in many other Christian communions, comes out very clearly if the Coronation service of the British monarch is looked at in the context of an ecumenical understanding of the Christian faith. It may be significant that, apparently, this has never been done.[7] In many ways, the Coronation service expresses what is most distinctive in Anglicanism at its splendid best. No other church in Christendom could have undertaken and carried off such a magnificent occasion, in which sincere devotion and dedication are combined with a sense of celebration and display of the most opulent worldly splendour and in which archaic forms are charged with a depth of meaning which no self-conscious attempt at contemporary relevance could achieve. It is not only because it was so widely visible on television that the Coronation of Queen Elizabeth II became perhaps the most universally impressive ceremonial event in history. Obviously, it was given poignancy by the noble dignity of the young queen, and 1953 was a good year in which to hold it, with the country recently emerging from a long war in which the loyalty and sense of unity of the overwhelming majority of the people had been consolidated and in which ties of kinship with most of the Commonwealth and the USA had been strengthened. If it had taken place fifteen years later, the mood would have been very different. Still, it is worth recalling today, when there is so much talk of 'secularization', that the impact of this 'sacralizing' event which took place only yesterday was so profound and so widespread. There was hardly a murmur of dissent. The voice of the rationalist, and still less that of the professional satirist, was not to be heard in the land and it was difficult even to gain a hearing for religious or cultural misgivings.

From the point of view of this argument, however, what was most noteworthy was that the Church of England appeared simply to take the service, the occasion, and its own part in it, entirely for granted. The ecclesiastical participants gave every evidence of enjoying themselves thoroughly. This was a great occasion of the English people and the English church, in which they were entirely at home. The nature of the service was, of course, fully explained to the public and Professor E. C. Ratcliffe produced an exemplary account of its history.[8] The then Archbishop of Canterbury, and other dignitaries, published discourses about the implication of the service for English life which, with the best will in the world, would have to be described as conventional and predictable. What was not undertaken was any effort to submit the Coronation service to re-examination from a theological point of view, both for the satisfaction of the conscience of the Church of England and for the reassurance of the rest of Christendom.

This is the more strange, and the more alarming, because in sharp contrast to the present time, the early 1950s were a period of relatively lively theological activity. It was not that people were incompetent to raise questions of principle or that, if they had, very few others would have been interested. More than that, with the lessons of the German church struggle still vividly before us and with the influence of Reinhold Niebuhr and his insight into the ambiguities of all forms of power at its peak, it would have seemed that the English Coronation service stood in urgent need of a great deal of theological justification.

First of all, there are the most obvious and general points. The reasons for the coronation of a monarch by representatives of the church in the context of a Christian service, when the country over which she reigns is highly pluralistic in religious allegiance and where the majority of the inhabitants pay little attention to the church, needs some explanation. The whole operation can hardly be taken for granted at this time of day. Also, as has already been partly indicated, the dangers of giving Christian sanction to assertions of national identity without a great deal of careful qualification have always been present, but the experiences of Germany and Japan had recently underlined them vividly. It may well be possible to give such explanations and to guard against such dangers. What is revealing about the Anglican mentality is that the Church of England did not appear under any internal compulsion to offer anything of the kind. What may turn out to be hardly less revealing is that other main-line churches of these islands appeared to take the situation as much for granted as did the Church of England. The only complaints came from some representatives of the Church of Scotland who grumbled that they did not have a sufficiently prominent part in the proceedings and who were, indeed, later moved to produce a pale reminiscence of the Coronation in St Giles.

But there are less obvious points which, from the point of view of the integrity of Christian institutions and their credibility to themselves, are certainly no less important. It is the responsibility of those who organize the worship of the church to make the symbols they use correspond as closely as possible to the realities they represent. Part of the point of worship lies precisely in that it is an attempt to move back into a situation where we can strive to reknit symbols and reality, because under the pressure of daily living in an imperfect world they are always being driven apart.

The real power of the monarchy in England has progressively diminished while actual power, and much of the authority that goes with it, lies elsewhere. If a coronation service under modern conditions is to be considered a legitimate activity from the point of view of the Christian church, that church must make the effort to see how it can be adapted so that its form expresses more adequately the relation between the monarch and the actual disposition of power and authority within the nation, or more accurately the group of nations involved. To do this would certainly be an exercise of great skill, tact and delicacy. It is, however, managed, and managed with all these qualities, in everyday relations between the Queen, her ministers and Parliament, and it is hard to believe that a church so sensitive to the need for cautious change while retaining historical continuity and so adept at producing dignified ritual as the Church of England could find it beyond its capacity. As far as can be known, not a finger was lifted by the leaders of the Church of England to make representation in the appropriate quarters that the Coronation service should be revised, except on such minor points as the degree of participation of representatives of other churches.

If it be argued, with the cynical and the indifferent, that the matter is of no account because the service is only a pageant anyway and that its charm lies in its archaic lack of relation to life, this is a line which cannot be accepted by the Church of England. Apart from anything else, it is belied by the facts. Not only does the ceremony itself still have important legal and moral significance, but the Coronation of Queen Elizabeth II was regarded by the Queen herself and the vast majority of her subjects, as well as by the church, as an act of peculiarly solemn dedication. But for the churchman there is an even weightier reason for rejecting this argument. The Coronation takes place in the context of the communion service of the Church of England. Nowhere on this earth is it more important to strive to keep close to the real world and to authentic relationships than here. Did the leaders do their duty by the church, by the monarch and by the people of Britain in accepting their role in this matter with such easy-going traditionalism? And did the leaders of the other churches, especially those of the Protestant Reformation, fulfil their duty by failing to call the attention of the Church of England to this matter?

Any discussion of the institution of the monarchy tends to engender more heat than light and there are those who regard all attempts to suggest modification of any aspect of it as a form of treason. It is important that the issue of the Coronation service be considered quietly and dispassionately, in the wide context of the matter of England and the matter of Britain as a whole and of the relation of monarchy and nation to the Christian faith. Personalities need not enter it, except in so far as we are fortunate in being at a moment in history when we have a popular queen in middle life and an heir to the throne who is himself a thoughtful Christian, which should make discussion all the easier. Does the Church of England still believe that 'there is a divinity which doth hedge a king'? If so, in what sense, and how, is it related to the government of England and of those nations which share that government without sharing the Anglican view of the monarchy? Where does the supreme governorship of the Church of England lie, in the person of the monarch, or, as the patronage system seems to imply, in the Queen in Parliament? What, if anything, is the rationale of the monarch's differing functions in relation to the Church of England and the Church of Scotland and where, if anywhere, does the monarch stand in relation to the church life of Wales? What is the position of the monarchy in an ecumenical age where churches recognize their mutual dependence? And where does the Commonwealth find its place in all this?

If the monarch, and the monarch in Parliament, were to protest that these questions are so obscure and so difficult to answer that they dare not raise them, that attitude would be understandable. But this makes it all the more essential for the Christian community to raise them. It is true that responsibility for determining these things, as for the arrangements for the Coronation service itself, do not rest with the Church of England alone, but the church has perfect freedom to make its views known, and the other parties involved would probably be grateful for help from the church in clarifying a situation whose confusion is becoming increasingly embarrassing. The Church of England must bear a very heavy load of responsibility for allowing a situation of such extraordinary vagueness and uncertainty to develop, so that there is little left for anyone to do but fall back upon the comparative safety of precedent. It is almost incredible that, although there have been no less than five commissions appointed by the church on church and state in the course of the last century or so, with many distinguished members, we seem to be no further forward. The danger is that when a situation is allowed to drift on while great changes take place all round, a crisis might arise when the whole apparatus of relationship between church and state will be swept away in a moment, with no genuine recent tests having been made to check whether the links between them are any longer capable of standing any serious strain.[9]

This matter is dwelt on not only because of its almost total neglect and inherent importance, but because it provides the most vivid illustration of the confusion about identity which exists in the predominant Anglican mentality and of the deep reluctance which exists to admit this, let alone to do anything about it. There are two questions about which the people of England, and, in particular the Church of England, must make up their minds if the future relations between the nations who make up the British people are to be sorted out on a constructive basis and a long-term strategy devised for the Christian community in its attitude to the wider community. What is the relation of this peculiar English-Anglican heritage and self-consciousness to the universal faith of Christendom, both Catholic and Protestant? And what is the role of the overt Christian community, those people in Britain who are prepared to acknowledge that their first loyalty is to that universal Christian faith rather than to their own denomination within these islands, to that peculiar heritage and self-consciousness?

This English and Anglican attitude, whose ambiguity is brought out in the Coronation service but which pervades the whole life of the church, is what makes the Church of England look to many people in the world like an agent of English nationalism rather than a part of the universal church. It helps to account for its singular failure, despite its aspirations to do so, to act as a bridge between Catholicism and the churches of the Protestant Reformation, except partially through its relation with churches of the Orthodox East, and to explain why it appears eccentric rather than more representative than anyone else among the churches of Christendom. It is one of the chief reasons why it is only too easy to produce an account of Anglicanism from the outside which places it in a very unattractive light. This may be worth doing partly, perhaps, to get out into the open, and therefore, out of the system, some of the resentment which any sensitive Free Churchman still feels about the pretensions of the Church of England and partly also, and more usefully, to help Anglicans see why they often arouse among non-English Christians in these islands surprisingly bitter animosity. This animosity was expressed with astonishing venom in the regrettable book *Power without Glory* by the late Professor Ian Henderson of Glasgow,[10] a man otherwise notable for shrewd judgment. The Church of England has many admirers and many more who treat it with a certain casual tolerance, but its relaxed and easy-going temperament should not make it underestimate the depth of the disapproval, and occasional abhorrence, with which it is viewed in some quarters, Christian as well as non-Christian.

In view of the hard things which are going to be said, they should be prefaced by the statement that they are not the expression of a personal point of view. Few people outside the Church of England can have more cause for personal gratitude to it than I, and few can have been treated by Anglicans with more consideration. One of my most fervent hopes is that I shall live to see the day when my own church is reunited with the Church of England. It will also be clear as the argument proceeds that, as far as I am concerned, what can be said against the Church of England is neither the whole truth nor the most important part of the truth.

Many people in the world suspect, and some believe, that the Church of England is little more than a thinly-disguised adaptation and distortion of the Christian faith to serve the purpose of English nationalism, and English nationalism at its most self-satisfied, uncritical and sanctimonious. When all the wraps are taken off it, the state connection which, despite all they say to the contrary, most Anglicans cherish as the most important thing about their church, is a way of ensuring that the church is always managed by people who are likely to be more loyal to English self-interest than to Christ, and to the traditional 'ruling-class' conception of that self-interest at that. The question as to who actually does the appointing of people to major office is unimportant since the whole system operates in such a way that the same kind of people will be appointed anyway. The spirit and the form of worship of the church are Erastian through and through, encouraging an attitude of self-congratulation on the part of some and servility by others in relation to the Royal Family and all the conservative forms of power and privilege which gather round them. As an Anglican himself said in a moment of unusually frank self-criticism as long ago as 1830:

> But our Church bears, and has ever borne, the marks of her birth. The child of regal and aristocratic selfishness and unprincipled tyranny, she has never dared to speak boldly to the great, but has contented herself with lecturing to the poor.[11]

Similarly, the Anglican justification of episcopacy, while solemnly couched in historical and theological terms, is better understood in practice as a convenient device for ensuring that, whatever happens in reunion but especially in home reunion, their own ruling clique will be in control, to ensure that nothing is done to alter the essential 'Englishness' of the church as that is defined in terms acceptable to the traditional 'ruling classes'. It is on a par with the proposal of those archetypal Anglican institutions, the church-associated public schools, to grant to local authorities the privilege of paying fees at public expense, on a scale set by the schools, for pupils chosen by the schools who will be of such a type and in such numbers as to ensure that nothing significant is changed in the school's style and character. The modernation and sobriety of Aglicanism, so much praised, in suitably moderate terms, by its own apologists to the detriment of other systems, is no more than the safe domestication of the potentially disturbing Christian faith within the cosy framework of English upper- and upper-middle-class life and that of its contented dependents. On the other hand, the alleged comprehensiveness of Anglicanism is more visible to those inside the Anglican fold than to those outside it. It is a way of saying to its own members, 'We do not mind what you believe as a matter of personal eccentricity—England has always prided itself on having a place for eccentrics—as long as you do nothing seriously to impair the Church of England in its Englishness.' At the same time, the doctrine of 'comprehensiveness' provides a convenient device for evading difficult issues and for drifting along by avoiding any decision which may demand a sacrifice or a painful break. Whether it is true or not that the British nation survives simply by 'muddling through', it is unquestionably true that this is how the Church of England manages to continue to exist. If one were looking for the best example that the world can provide of Christianized paganism, of the worship of the gods of hearth and home by those to whom the lines are fallen in pleasant places, there is no need to look beyond the Church of England. Let anyone consider the monuments in, for example, Westminster Abbey or Exeter Cathedral, not to say a host of patrician country churches, and deny it.

This may partly account for the fact that the Church of England is the most snobbish church in Christendom. The word 'snobbish' is used advisedly at this point. The vices on this level of bodies whose beliefs are passionately held and who draw sharp distinctions between themselves and others who are their rivals because they have to struggle hard against them to maintain their identity and their power, are bigotry and intolerance. The Church of England has not been in that position except in a few moments in her life, such as the seventeenth century, when she has not been slow to display these vices. Snobbery is the vice of those who have long enjoyed power and privilege without serious effort and who have come to afford to be relaxed and subtle about their superiority, gently but firmly keeping in their subordinate place those who are inexperienced enough to try to imitate them without having first received the stamp of their approval or impertinent enough even to assert their independence in what the privileged have been accustomed to assume is their own domain. The 'upper-class' English have long been adept at doing this in the field of ordinary social relations and members of the Church of England have been no less adept at doing it in the ecclesiastical field. Like all snobs, they congratulate themselves that they are able to get on much better with the ecclesiastical working classes, with Italian Catholic peasants or the Salvation Army, than with the ecclesiastical petite-bourgeoisie, with Baptists or American Methodists, without stopping for a moment to ask themselves why.

Not the least of the indictments against the Church of England is that it has been a major element in making England such a very class-conscious country, especially since Anglican conservative groups reasserted their sway over many of its social and cultural institutions after the first impact of the Industrial Revolution had spent itself in the nineteenth century and had produced large numbers of wealthy recruits for the propertied classes. The cause of Christianity in England would be in much worse case even than it is today, and the alienation of many manual workers and liberally-minded members of the middle classes would be even more complete, if there had not been, throughout this period, many English Christians who rejected the Church of England and its view of society and who were prepared to fight for the political and social rights of those who were not 'top people' in Anglican eyes and who were also prepared to work out forms of Christian nurture and social life and responsibility which were free from patronage, servility and indolent traditionalism. If England never became a country like pre-revolutionary France, no thanks were due to the Church of England. By the mercy of God, there has always been another England which, at crucial moments in the nation's history, has either been able to assert its will or at least compel the ruling groups to keep other options open. In modern times also, there have been the Scots and the Welsh, who have brought the stimulus of a different way of looking at things into English life itself. 1660, and the church settlement of 1662 which followed it, was a victory, not without its due measure of chicanery, for one power group over others in English life, which effectively disfranchised large sections of the community and made a rift in the Christian community life of England which has even yet not been fully repaired. 1688 represented a modification of the situation and many others have taken place since, but the full implications of the rift have never been honestly faced, with the result that the Church of England has never been in a position to exercise a genuine ministry of reconciliation. From the point of view of the unity of the nation, England has never had a truly established church since 1662, or, for that matter, since the outbreak of the Civil War. What it has had is one Christian denomination, for most of the time more powerful than all the others put together, which has jealously guarded and kept it to itself all the privileges of an established church while it has often, and, in recent times progressively, shed its responsibilities. How, without self-deception, has the Anglican parson ever since been able to justify his traditional claim to be the 'person' of his parish when, in the most vigorous and forward-looking parts of England, large numbers of Christians, at least as serious in their commitment and as socially responsible as the majority of those who accepted his ministrations, were able to maintain themselves in ordered Christian communities from one generation to the next without the benefit of those ministrations?

This is the great weakness of Maurice's *Kingdom of Christ*, which is still the most substantial Anglican attempt to come to terms with Dissenters and to put intelligent questions to them about the issues involved in a church's attempt to serve a whole community in such a way as to express what it means in that place to represent the universal kingdom of Christ. Like so many other converts, understandably taken up with his own vision of what the church might be at its best, he does not allow sufficiently for the fact that, to those outside, the Church of England does not begin to look like a truly national church but only like one particularly arrogant and domineering Christian denomination, interested only in itself, and determined to hold on to its power and privileges at all costs. If it were serious about being a national church, it would show a sensitive concern for the well-being of dissident Christians within its nation which, until recently, only a few rare spirits in its midst have ever expressed.

Let it now also be said, with equal emphasis and with, I hope, even greater conviction, that all this is not the whole truth and not the most relevant and important part of the truth which needs attention today. Some might still feel that it would have been best not to say it and to let the dead bury their dead. The trouble is that, greatly diminished though they may fortunately be, these old controversies are not yet quite dead and, even when they are, their memory lives after them and poisons the present unless it is brought into the open and dealt with. Many Anglicans still have to be made to see that they really do have a serious problem in their relations with other Christians, especially other Christians within these islands. It is simply not enough for them to believe, as many of them still do believe even in the post-Fisher era, that these problems will solve themselves if approached with an amiable pragmatism which involves little adjustment on their part. Yet this has to be said so strongly just because the Church of England is by far the greatest Christian institution in these islands. It is inconceivable that the common life of Britain could be re-Christianized without it. It is also true that, despite all the limitations so faithfully described in the last few paragraphs, the Church of England has nevertheless managed to nurture Christian gifts and graces, many of them unique to herself, which have enormously enriched the whole church of Christ in these islands and throughout the world. More than that, it has acted as a leaven in the life of the whole community, often when it has been least conscious of itself as the Church of England, which has helped to give English life many of its most characteristic virtues.

It should be remembered that the organic conception of their institutions which English people have, and which the Church of England exemplifies more clearly than any other, means that it is to be expected that the English church would be a particularly mixed institution, one in which the wheat and the tares, the flowers and the weeds, the dead wood and the living branches, or whatever other appropriately horticultural metaphor lies to hand, will be allowed to grow together with great freedom. 'The godly discipline' of the Calvinist Reformation has never sat easily upon English shoulders, and when the very peculiar situation of the Church of England in relation to the national life is borne in mind, what becomes most impressive is not that there should be so many tares among the wheat but that there should be so much healthy wheat among those tares, so many precious flowers among the weeds, so many living branches, or at least sturdy pieces of timber, among the dead wood.

We have seen that the Christian church rarely measures up to all the problems which arise when she actually becomes a successful institution in the world. It could be claimed that the Church of England has been the most successful large-scale church the world has ever seen. It may not look like that today as compared with, for example, some of the American churches, but if it is looked at over the space of the last four hundred years, or even the last thousand years or more, the justice of the claim becomes more obvious. Granting all the failures which have been described, it has yet managed to remain for generation after generation in close association with the 'commanding heights' of the national life without ever completely succumbing to the corrupting influence of power, and while it has never been its style to produce spectacular saints, it has nourished in every generation large numbers of people, clerical and lay, of remarkable sweetness, grace and unobtrusive personal humility. Throughout the centuries, it has been a great and rich and conservative institution without the rigidity and reactionary defensiveness of Latin Christendom, whether in Italy or Spain or France. It has been one of the most deeply nationalistic churches in the world, yet it has been free of the religious fossilization and uncritical identification with a narrowly-conceived national interest to which most Orthodox churches have succumbed, while it has also succeeded in persuading many people of different race and culture from its own to enter into communion with it. If it has not been notable for its ability to initiate changes and to produce new ideas out of its own life, it has, with all its inevitable conservatism, proved its ability to respond to changes without evaporating either into sentimentality or secularity. This is a fate which many of the more free Protestant churches seem unable to avoid when they have been in existence for more than a few generations. Among the established churches of the world, only a few of the older Reformed churches, such as those of Holland, Scotland and parts of Switzerland, can compare with the Church of England in maintaining over a long period this combination of social dominance with religious vitality and readiness to change.

It is not fashionable to take any pride in such achievements in these days, and this makes it easy to ignore the significance of the success of the Church of England in maintaining the rich and powerful in Christian allegiance. She may have left other churches to stimulate and nourish new social groups, and has never been either gracious or scrupulous about the ways in which she tries to seduce members of those groups from their old allegiance once they achieve social prominence, yet there has been a persistent leaven at work in Anglicanism to prevent the corrupting influences of wealth and power from having things their own way. Monstrous inequalities of income and status as between members of the clergy themselves have been allowed at various times in the life of the church, again partly as a result of the church's very social success which meant that honours and privileges were heaped upon her leaders, but determined efforts have also been made to reduce them. Today, the relative social and financial positions of the clergy of the Church of England to each other are better balanced than they have ever been. The amount of complacent acceptance of privilege, with its attendant snobbery, within the Church of England has been sufficiently dwelt on in this discussion. What strikes the eye less obviously is the cheerfulness with which its clergy accept their lot when their privileges diminish or they have none. This became visible in the long years after the Second World War, when all clerical incomes fell badly behind most others in the inflationary race, until the activities of the Church Commissioners and Christian Stewardship campaigns began to make up some of the leeway.[12] Allied to that is a peculiarly attractive distrust of self-seeking and self-advertisement which, at its best, is far more interested in ensuring that what is right is done with the minimum of disturbance and contention than in obtaining credit for the doer. When the Anglican identification with conservative English attitudes and institutions is expressed with personal humility, its quiet pastoral diligence is not only beautiful to observe but does much to explain the secret of the persistence throughout the centuries of those attitudes and institutions. The dignified seemliness of most Anglican buildings and the church's almost instinctive sense of restrained beauty in the conduct of public worship are no mere veneer. They express what is most authentic and most attractive in the Anglican spirit at its best.

Any group which becomes successful is rarely entirely admirable and naturally arouses resentment among its rivals or among others at whose expense it enjoys success. It is hardly surprising that the English, who have continued to be extremely successful for a relatively long time, should have unattractive traits and that they should arouse resentment. Yet it has not been the most devotedly Anglican of them who have been the most unattractive or the most resented, and the best of them have probably been less resented than the members of almost any other 'top nation' in history. This becomes particularly clear when it is remembered that there are other Anglicans than the clergy. The clergy of any church are an ambiguous group, with their own good and bad professional characteristics. It is a sign of maturity on the part of the clergyman that he should allow for this and not be surprised by the uneasy and mixed reaction most people have towards him in fulfilling his complex social role. In fact, it has been one of the weaknesses of the Anglican clergy that they have had difficulty in realizing this, so that many have been over-eager to receive social acceptance. But the English 'gentleman' who is, at the same time, a sincerely practising Anglican must be one of the most truly gentle of men ever to exercise great power. The amount of educational effort and social training required to make him so gentle while yet so powerful should not be underestimated. It owes not a little to the clergy and to his other tutors. It probably owes more to those godly wives and mothers and aunts who have always been, much more than her

Prayer Book and her parish churches, 'the greatest glory of the Church of England', and who are the most devoted and discriminating, if not always the most appreciated, participants in her life.

More than that, it is worth remembering that at the very time when English power and her pride of empire were at their greatest the Church of England was at her most earnest and hard-working, even though not perhaps, at her most self-critical. For all the stuffiness and snobbery of Victorian Anglicanism, the church at that time was in the process of recovering her soul. Trollope's Barchester novels probably give a reliable picture of the outlook and attitude of average, not particularly reflective or profound, clergy and laity in a conservative area of mid-Victorian England, but they are far from representing the Church of England in all its many aspects at the time. In particular, they ignore the religious intensity and the questioning, doubting spirit which were characteristic of the creative and innovative minorities in the church.

The paradoxical truth is that it is this religious intensity which both saved the soul of the Church of England and did so at the price of making her increasingly indifferent to the matter of England. It found its chief expression in two movements, Evangelicalism and Anglo-Catholicism, which gave new depth to the Anglican spirit but drained away much of the vitality which might have gone into redefining the role of the established church in relation to the rest of the nation in a rapidly changing world.

This is not to say that either of these religious movements lacked social consequences. No intense religious movement at the heart of a community can be without them, even though many of them may be indirect and the connection with what gave them their start may not be readily discernible. The direct social consequence of nineteenth-century Evangelicalism was undoubtedly deeply conservative, in turning people's minds away from the critical analysis of the society in which they were set and encouraging them to take the structures and the distribution of power within them for granted at a time when they were changing rapidly and badly needed critical examination. This was culpable, in the way that similar attitudes among many present-day Evangelicals are culpable. A conservative bias is not the same as a Christian attitude. Yet its indirect effects were more constructive, and in the long run more important. Whatever it did to his public life, there was no question that Evangelicalism did 'interfere with a man's private life'. It trained large and important sections of the community, some rich and many not so rich and not a few of the poor, in habits of self-discipline and personal responsiblity. This had immediate effects on the quality of family life, and from this its influence flowed out into wider social relationships. It produced a compassionate and determined conscience which stirred people first to campaign against the more glaringly scandalous of social ills, of which slavery and the exploitation of child labour were the most obvious, and as time went on it extended itself to a much wider range of social concerns. A great deal of reformist zeal in English life can be traced to an Evangelical root, whether Anglican or Free Church, even though it may sometimes be necessary to go back more than one generation to find it.

The social impact of Anglo-Catholicism has been more limited, despite its well-known connection with the Christian Socialist movement and the dedicated activity of a small number of priests among the urbanized poor. It had a smaller base as a popular movement and much of its appeal lay in its being a romantic reaction against the Industrial Revolution and the modern world on the part of those who were fortunate enough to be able to enjoy the best of the old order. All the same, as some of its monuments like Butterfield's All Saints, Margaret Street, reveal, it brought much needed intensity and depth to English religion and helped Anglicanism resist its perennial temptation to adjust itself uncritically to whatever is the dominant fashion of the time. And it has enabled some Englishmen, including not a few of those closely involved with public affairs, to find a critique of their own society which is more genuinely conservative than that of the so-called Conservative party, which tends to identify the English heritage with that of the interests of the last generation of Englishmen to have made a good deal of money.

These movements did have social consequences, therefore, but the fact that so much imaginative religious energy went into them meant that there was little left over to infuse the Broad Church ideal with power to find a more generous vision of England. The result was that the alternative to Evangelicalism and Anglo-Catholicism has too often seemed to be only that conventional and safely calculable 'C of E' Establishment-mindedness which, as even Maurice had to acknowledge, has always remained the dominant popular Anglican attitude.[13] Yet the possibility of its being more than this has always been open, and it is vital to put the best interpretation upon it because it seems to provide the only hope of giving Anglicanism a continuing basis for its existence as an established church.

The thinker who was the most self-conscious and articulate exponent of the Broad Church ideal was Coleridge. He had the great merit not merely of seeing what the social and intellectual role of a national church should be but also how it should be related to the Christian gospel, which he was careful not to identify with it. Arnold exemplified it in a more activist form, and the early public school ideal as he understood it was an attempt to begin to give expression to it on the level of education. The decline of that ideal into one of 'muscular Christianity' and complacent patriotism has been described in David Newsome's *Godliness and Good Learning*,[14] and the public schools have taken a great deal of punishment from the more disgruntled of their products ever since, much of it no doubt justified. It is worth remembering, however, that the best elements of the Arnold tradition have continued as a leaven in British life to this day. R. H. Tawney and William Temple are outstanding examples of the Rugbeians who, among others of similar background, have expressed in public and private life the kind of ideal for which Arnold worked.

In fact, even allowing for the energy which went into Evangelicalism and Anglo-Catholicism, it is curious that the Broad Church movement did not capture the imagination of more Englishmen than it did. Maurice, its theologian, failed to catch the public ear on a sufficient scale and there was no adequate popularizer. Kingsley might have been, but he lacked theological depth and sensitivity, although it is interesting and may be significant that he had considerable influence among Dissenters and Methodists.[15] If the Broad Church position was to succeed, it had to differentiate itself sufficiently from merely conventional Anglicanism to provide a basis for Anglican self-criticism and for a prophetic attitude to society. Perhaps the chief reason why this never happened was that its most alert and vigorous heirs as the nineteenth moved into the twentieth century became theological liberals and, in some cases, 'modernists'. These certainly performed some of the functions of Coleridge's 'clerisy', but only at the price of losing much that was distinctive in their point of view, especially as the non-clerical educated classes were beginning their enormous expansion at the same time. It is, perhaps, easy to underestimate the value of the work done for English life by the Anglican liberals and the modernists of the last generation. Many of the articles in *The Modern Churchman* between the wars about social and political matters still read very well, even if the same cannot be said about the theological ones, and, with the exception of a few crusty conservatives like Dean Inge, they were rarely far from the most enlightened movements of social reform in their time. What they lacked was a profound enough Christian analysis of human nature and institutions to make them really effective either in national leadership or in Anglican self-criticism.

It may turn out to be very significant that the theologian who represented a position most like that to which Broad Churchmen might have aspired in English life at the end of the nineteenth and in the early twentieth centuries was not an Anglican at all but a Congregationalist and a Scot, P. T. Forsyth, especially in his books *Theology in Church and State* (1915), *The Justification of God* (1916) and *The Principle of Authority* (1913).[16] He created a great deal of bewilderment in his own time, not least among those of his own denomination, but he maintained an awareness of the judgments of God in the affairs of men and of the greatness of his kingdom which reflected itself in a very strong 'public sense' and a power of prophetic utterance which were sadly lacking in much of the Anglican and Free Church life of his time. There may also be something to build on for the future shape of the Christian community in England in the fact that two of the best exponents in their teaching and in their practice of something near to Maurice's, and Coleridge's, view of the Kingdom of Christ were not Anglicans but Congregationalists, Philip Doddridge of Northampton in the eighteenth century, whom Maurice would have loved, and R. W. Dale of Birmingham in the nineteenth, who loved Maurice.

All this is far from saying that the Broad Church tradition in this sense has not been a significant influence in the Church of England over the last century, still less that it is incapable of revival. It was a strong element in colouring the Anglo-Catholicism of the Christendom group, and its influence could be detected even in such an establishmentarian as Bishop Hensley Henson, the conventionality of whose Anglican judgments was modified not only by the distinction of his literary style but also by that sharpness of social observation which made him believe that Anglican establishment must end. William Temple might be held to be the outstanding representative of this tradition in the twentieth century, and he was outstanding enough, but he never seemed quite to acquire the necessary critical self-consciousness about England and its characteristic life which the situation demanded, despite his concern both for church reform and for Christian social action. There were signs in his last days that he was reaching for it, as he came to learn from the rise of Nazism and the teaching of Reinhold Niebuhr more about the ambiguities of human institutions and human motives than his essentially conservative mind had previously enabled him to see.[17] And through the works of A. R. Vidler, Archbishop Lord Ramsey and several others, the work of Maurice has come to be appreciated as never before, although perhaps he is still admired more than he is followed.[18]

Yet even if the possibility of a revival of the great tradition of Coleridge, Maurice and Arnold remains, the Church of England in general seems to have lost heart about ever being again the Church of the English people in their sense. When Mr Simon Raven, in his curiously ambivalent book on *The English Gentleman*, said, 'If ever there was an irrelevance in English life, it has been, since 1918, the Church of England',[19] he was speaking demonstrable nonsense. It was an observation almost on a par with the famous remark of Sir George Sitwell to Evelyn Waugh when, sitting on a terrace at Renishaw and overlooking the crowded industrial valley below, he said, 'You see, there is no one between us and the Locker-Lampsons.' Yet Mr Raven was probably giving expression to the widespread feeling among those large sections of the community who are careful to move only among those of their own kind who echo each other's opinions that, whereas to be Anglican was once part of the definition of an Englishman, and especially an English gentleman, it is no longer so. What is surprising, despite a great deal of evidence to the contrary since 1918, such as the Prayer Book debates, the abdication crisis, the Coronation, the Princess Margaret–Peter Townshend matter and many less publicized issues, is the extent to which the Church of England itself has come to agree with this evaluation of its position.

Is it entirely out of order for a British Dissenter to protest that this is simply not good enough? The Church of England is committed to trying to be the established church of the English people and, over a long history, has inescapably contracted certain responsibilities to that people. Simply to sidle quietly out of the responsibilities of establishment is the most craven way to go. It is the attitude of someone who, as he grows older, finds that the burdens and complications of marriage are greater and the children more demanding than they have been in the past and who, therefore, wants to phase out the relationship with the minimum amount of unpleasantness, so that he can enjoy a peaceful old age. If England is ceasing any longer to be in any significant sense Christian England, the Church of England has the duty of confronting the government and people of England not only with the obligation to redefine the relation between church and state but also with the question of what they now mean by the bond of loyalty which holds the English people together. She would have to do this with a very clear recognition that she herself has allowed the situation in relation to establishment to drift on for so long and so aimlessly that state and church are now in an almost impenetrable fog about where the characteristic institutions of the nation stand in relation to Christian faith. These institutions do not exist simply as natural facts. They are neither self-generating nor self-justifying. They are based on assumptions about human nature and destiny. It is the duty of a national church to remind people constantly about those assumptions and to submit them to critical scrutiny as the first step towards any re-ordering of those institutions in a changing world. The Church of England will be false to her best genius and remove whatever justification exists for all the privileges she has enjoyed throughout her history if she is content to give up her peculiar relation to the English state without facing as a Christian community all the issues involved for herself in such an action and without also trying to make the rest of the nation face the issues involved for the nation as a whole.

If she fails to do this, it will not happen, as so many advocates of disestablishment argue, that the Church of England would simply regain her freedom to minister to the nation in new ways. The present arrangement limits that freedom only marginally. What would be much more likely is that large areas of her life would fade into the amiable and nostalgic dimness of a body like the Church of Ireland in our time. But that would not be the whole story, for the Church of England has been too much involved for that to happen over the whole of her life. What would also happen would be that the things which the Church of England has done well in the past will no longer be done, with grave social consequences. If she gives up trying to help those in authority avoid the corrupting influence of power, and contents herself with being the domestic chaplain of those who once held power, along with their retainers, she and they will decline into a querulous and lonely old age while those in real power go their own way. It would be terrible for England, as well as for the Church of England, if the typical Anglican became someone like Charles Ryder in Evelyn Waugh's *Brideshead Revisited*, seeing the Christian faith only as the repository of an idealized past and finding a perverse satisfaction in failure, because there is nothing to admire in the present and nothing in this life to hope for in the future.

This need not be the Anglican fate, nor do I believe that it will be. It is, after all, significant that Evelyn Waugh, and others who felt like him, had to become Roman Catholics after their own curious fashion in order to find a congenial environment for their nostalgia, although even there they quickly found too much vitality for their comfort. No one could be more Anglican than Sir John Betjeman, yet his nostalgia is kept firmly in proportion by a living Christian faith, a breadth of sympathy and a love of English life and ways so strong that it leads him on from cherishing the treasures of the past to seeing the virtues of the present and wanting to do something about our having a worth-while future. It was not an accident either that T. S. Eliot, a convert to Anglicanism from New England, who was attracted to it precisely because of its traditionalism and its difference from the modern world, became markedly more open and co-operative in his Christian sympathies as he grew older. The Church of England will not settle for becoming an upper-class sect, resenting the present and fearing the future, 'a decayed gentlewoman'. She touches life at too many points, is too wisely led in these days, too committed to reunion and too active in intelligent reorganization and redeployment for that to happen. But she may miss many of the opportunities of effective influence which are open to her in the common life of England and of Britain as a whole unless she resists her present tendency to regard being established as a burden to be shrugged off rather than an inescapable responsibility which she has inherited, and which has been a major factor in making her what she is.

It is not in dispute among Christians that if churches are to fulfil their function in the world, they have to retain in their own hands their freedom to prophesy to society and the freedom to go against the state and other dominant institutions of society should the need arise. That these freedoms are inadequately safeguarded in the Church of England, Dissenters have always maintained, but Anglicanism has justified its position on the ground of the special relation which is alleged to exist between the English state and the church through the person of the monarch and the principle of continuity and organic growth which this relation expresses. If the Church of England wants to change her mind about this, those of us who were never convinced by this argument can sympathize, but that sympathy will be greatly diminished if what she now wishes to do is simply to shuffle out of her responsibility for all that has been bound up with this special relationship and to settle simply for being one Christian denomination among others, while still enjoying the afterglow of establishment in her beautiful churches. Anglicanism is bound up with being English, and the Church of England must help the people of England face honestly the problems of national identity in relation to Christian faith in the setting of the modern world. The argument of this book is that this cannot any longer be done in English terms alone. It must be done in an ecumenical context and in relation to the much larger and long-neglected question of what it means to be British in a Christian way. But it will not begin to be done unless the Church of England discovers a new and much more critical self-consciousness about its own peculiar position as the established church of the English nation.

3   The English Free Churches

It is a measure of the success of the Church of England in identifying itself with the dominant picture of England that, except in a few areas of the country, the Anglican religious tradition is thought by most people to be the only significant English religious tradition. This is particularly true of these who are not regular church-goers. It is not simply that the Church of England is the only church they stay away from. Most of them assume that it is the only church from which they can stay away, with the one big exception in these days of the Roman Catholic, which is for foreigners anyway. The more prominent and prosperous Free Churches, whose buildings sometimes look like those of Anglican churches, are often treated by such people, when they come to enquire about a rite of passage, as though they are the same as the Church of England and they are puzzled when they discover some differences and difficulties. On any showing, the Free Churches are important, if secondary, institutions in the life of England, at least comparable in social significance to, say, the public schools or the Liberal party. Yet when the publicly subsidized British Council produced during the war the series of books already mentioned called 'Britain in Pictures', it found room for one on *British Fairs and Circuses*, but for nothing on the Free Churches except one page at the end of a book on the Church of England. It probably never occurred to those who planned the series that the millions of Methodists, Baptists, Presbyterians and Congregationalists who live in the English-speaking world outside these islands might be interested, if indeed they were aware of the existence of those millions.

It is ironical that many Americans also make this assumption, ironical because some of the most characteristic and influential communities in America, notably those of New England and Pennsylvania, were settled by groups consciously protesting against this Anglican dominance of English life and wanting something different. The Massachusetts Bay colony was a deliberate and very fully worked-out attempt to build a new England across the seas which would be an example to the old England of what a commonwealth truly reformed according to the Word of God should be. William Penn's Pennsylvania also arose out of a rejection of the values, style and power structure of the old England. Throughout the nineteenth century, as Denis Brogan observed in his book on *The English People*,[20] which was written during the war for American readers, peculiarly strong links existed between the culture and style of life of white Anglo-Saxon Protestant Americans and the English Free Churches, as there also did with Scotland, Wales and Northern Ireland. But for many modern Americans, partly because so many latter-day articulate Anglophiles are students of English literature, England is the land of Eliot's 'Classicism, Royalism, Anglicanism', and anything which does not fit is ignored, a process strongly aided and abetted in these days by another public body, the British Tourist Authority.

This underplaying of the role of the Free Churches in the shaping of modern England cannot be without an element of deliberation, even though it may not always have been fully conscious. Old attitudes die very hard in English life. Most committed Anglicans today treat Free Churchmen as their Christian colleagues and neighbours as a matter of course, but there are still some slight social constraints between establishment-minded Englishmen and Free Churchmen and there remain blind spots, especially when matters of historical interpretation are concerned. An argument about the English Civil War can still become quite heated, and the story of the Free Churches in the nineteenth century reads very differently to many of their children from what it does to most Anglicans. The truth is that the Free Churches became so powerful in the nineteenth century that, for the first time since the seventeenth, they began seriously to threaten the hegemony of the Anglican establishment and to frighten them more than they found it expedient to admit even to themselves. The 1851 census revealed that, on that particular Sunday, more people were worshipping in non-Anglican churches than in Anglican, and those proportions remained fairly constant until decline began to set in towards the end of the century, while, despite the steady creaming-off of prosperous Nonconformists into the ranks of the establishment, the political power, educational standards and general prosperity of their churches increased. They expressed not only the outlook and aspirations of a different class from that of Anglican leadership but also an alternative vision of England and of what she might become. Their links with the early leaders of the Industrial Revolution and also with many of the most able and independent industrial workers themselves were incomparably stronger than were those of the Church of England, with its association with the landed gentry. As the century wore on, the Free Churches lost some of their religious vitality and distinctiveness, but became more and more the vehicles through which the aspirations of the new lower-middle classes for self-improvement, for greater participation in national affairs and for greater social recognition, found very full expression. A Congregational church in a typical London suburb at the turn of the century had a range of ancillary activities which anticipated nearly all the educational and social-service activities of the present day and not a few of the recreational ones. Accentuated by the controversy over the Education Act of 1902, all this built up to a climax in the great Liberal victory of 1906, which produced for the first time a non-Anglican majority in the House of Commons, and also incidentally, according to Denis Brogan, the ablest group of MPs ever to appear at Westminster. It must have looked to the more euphoric of Free Churchmen as though 1648, if not exactly 1649, had come again.

Why this should have turned out to be the end, rather than the beginning, of this new rule of the saints will be considered shortly. The point now to be made is that, if the Jacobite plots are discounted, this is the only threat that the old English Establishment has had to face since the seventeenth century and with it the prospect of the only 'alternative society' which has ever been a real option in this land. The Establishment reacted with every weapon of snobbery and social innuendo at its disposal, and the remnants of this attitude still linger on.

Like some other aspects of the English Establishment tradition, such as the contempt for anyone 'in trade' or the dogma that a public school education was the only one worthy of the name, this attitude found its strongest expression in the pàrticular circumstances of the nineteenth century and has largely passed away with the passing of that age. The damage it did to the Free Churches remained, however, and it is only slowly that they have shed its corrupting effects, as these churches move today into a situation much more like that which they knew in the eighteenth century than that in the nineteenth century. The fight to gain recognition in the face of the repressive tactics of the Establishment, both ecclesiastical and civil, gave them a stridency and militancy and a tendency to over-simplify issues in black and white which have now largely disappeared from their internal life, except where an unduly rhetorical sermonic style is still to be found, but they have had a powerful influence on the techniques of reformist groups and of the public media of communication, in which the children of Free Churches are to be found in large numbers. They were not the only religious influence, since Protestant revivalism, which is largely of American origin and is not to be identified with old-time Nonconformity, has also been an important factor, but they cannot be exempted from blame for using public demonstrations as forms of political pressure and slogans instead of argument which have become such a feature of the behaviour of the advocates of 'righteous causes' in our own time.[21]

Similar failings appeared on a deeper level. Nineteenth-century Nonconformity suffered from a certain gracelessness and lack of imaginative adventurousness, an aspiration after 'respectability' which made it content with the safe and the mediocre, and this remains as a powerful factor in its life to this day. When Matthew Arnold in *Culture and Anarchy* sneered at the Philistinism which was displayed pre-eminently by Nonconformists, he was speaking about something which was real enough. What made his 'superior person's' sarcasm so offensive was his failure to see, even though he was his father's son and an inspector of schools to boot, how much people like himself carried responsibility for their being like that. Nonconformist worship was impoverished, Nonconformist education was limited and utilitarian, Nonconformist social habits and styles were made either insecure or complacently provincial because the custodians of high culture in England, the clerisy, of whom Matthew Arnold was one of the chief, snubbed them at every turn and refused to have anything to do with them except at the price of the surrender of their convictions and their loyalties. And when, despite this, they managed to give their children a better education than they received themselves, these representatives of high culture, both clerical and lay, did their best to estrange them from their parents by sneering at their limitations and offering them a place in their world only if they would cut themselves off from their heritage.

The result of this has been that, after the brief flurry of assertiveness which reached its political climax in 1906 and then subsided, Free Churchmen have had a 'poor relation' mentality to English society and culture which still persists. They were intimidated into accepting the evaluation put upon them by their Victorian critics as a cross they had to bear and, in the perverse way in which things so often work, they often seem to have been at pains to prove that it was true. Indeed, in view of the responsibility which cultivated Anglicans must carry for having fostered this attitude, it is pleasant to be able to acknowledge that it has been such a typical Anglican as Sir John Betjeman, ably assisted by Mr John Piper, who has led latter-day Dissenters to an appreciation of parts of their own heritage which they themselves had often come to despise, such as many of their nineteenth-century church buildings. A growing number of Cambridge historians, not all of them Dissenters, have also helped them to see afresh how very constructive many aspects of their social and political activities in the nineteenth century were.[22] Mr Edward Thompson's account of Methodism at its most reactionary in the days of the egregious Jabez Bunting is far from telling the whole story.[23] It is, of course, wrong to think of the Free Churches, as many outsiders do, as all of one piece. They have much in common, but there are important differences, sometimes between different sections of the same denomination. Thus the differing streams within Methodism have been very marked, and are still influential, and the conservative evangelicals among the Baptists have more in common with Anglican evangelicals than they have with other Free Churchmen and even with some of their more liberal Baptist colleagues. Yet most of the Congregationalists, the Quakers, the Unitarians, who were much more numerous and influential in nineteenth-century England than they are now, and many Methodists and Baptists, shared a common vision of England which was generous and which was identified more closely with the aspirations of large numbers of ordinary people than any other social vision before or since.

Partly because of this, it was a vision which lacked imaginative colour. There was precious little of Merrie England and dancing around the maypole about it. It was too close to everyday reality in industrialized England for that. It found expression chiefly in idealistic preaching and public speaking (although, as David Martin has reminded us, the place of choral singing should not be underestimated),[24] and also in concrete schemes for social betterment either through politics or voluntary action by individuals. The latter was very important. Some of their achievements are now patronizingly described as paternalistic by those who prefer that the exercise of power should never be personalized, but it is hard to think of gentler and more humane parents than those who fathered such places as Bournville or the Garden City Movement, and in town councils throughout the land it was often enough Free Churchmen who were taking the lead in laying the infra-structure of the modern social services. In the first half of the nineteenth century, and for some a good deal later, this vision was disfigured by laissez-faire individualism and that severity to the undeserving poor which is often characteristic of individuals and groups struggling by their own efforts to move out of poverty themselves. Later in the nineteenth century, it succumbed either to a pacifist distrust of power and the responsibility which it brings or to populism. Yet that individualism, rugged as it sometimes may have been, was the expression of a determination to find a place in the world independently of the ruling classes with their ideology of 'my station and its duties', and the later populism was closely linked with respect for the ordinary man's right to express what he really believed when others would prefer him to think differently. We see today how easily 'democracy' tends to be denounced as 'populism' when the views of the majority no longer find favour with those who, while claiming to be democratic, would like to have the support of the majority against what they would claim to be the 'reactionary' views of the old ruling groups. And it should never be forgotten that the populism of the Free Churches in the later nineteenth century, for all the limitation of vision which made them unsympathetic to those who did not share their own prejudices and style of life, was very greatly mitigated by their desire for self-improvement. This is no less true of the very similar popular Free Church life of Scotland and America in the nineteenth century, which has received such unfavourable treatment from George Elder Davie in his *The Democratic Intellect*[25] and Richard Hofstadter in his *Anti-Intellectualism in American Life*.[26] By the standards of high culture, its achievements were unimpressive, but its own high standards of parental care and its recognition of the need for training and self-discipline created the context out of which large numbers of its children were able to move into the world of high culture. Only a little of it reacted into anti-intellectual fundamentalism, and hardly any did in England. Without it, it is hard to see how the vast expansion of higher education, on either side of the Atlantic, could ever have moved off the ground.

Mr Christopher Hill, who has taken a lead in helping us dispel misconceptions about the alleged obscurantism of the Puritanism of the seventeenth century, once described the difference between that Puritanism and later Nonconformity as that between wine and vinegar.[27] That is not fair. Only in some of its backwaters did nineteenth-century Nonconformity become vinegary. Apart from anything else, it quickly lost its tartness and became too sugary, as P. T. Forsyth never ceased to point out. Typical Nonconformity at its worst was rarely less palatable than home-brewed small beer, a characteristic it only too faithfully carried on into the twentieth century. At its best, it often achieved the level of a sound bourgeois growth, not altogether unworthy to stand beside the vintages of the seventeenth century. For example, the Congregational ministers of the larger churches of English provincial towns and suburbs never quite lost the old Puritan vision of the godly commonwealth, and some of them had a trace of the radicalism of the Fifth Monarchy men. There were very few worthwhile projects for social development or amelioration which they, and those like them in related denominations, did not do a great deal either to initiate or to support, and they gave more depth and sense of direction to social idealism than it would otherwise have possessed. Men like Dale and Dawson in Birmingham were outstanding, but they were representative of many rather than exceptional.[28] The drains, streets and schools of Birmingham and similar places may seem a long way from the reordering of English life under the Common-wealth, but the connection is there to be traced. And on less mundane levels, several of the most civilized institutions of the great industrial cities of England, their libraries, Athenaeums and concert halls, owed a good deal in their origins to the democratically based zeal for a richer and nobler life of the despised Dissenters. They did more to propagate 'sweetness and light' in some singularly dark places than Matthew Arnold, who seemed to know more about provincial France than about provincial England, ever gave them credit for.

The main question confronting Free Churchmen concerning their social role today—they may have no less important questions to face concerning faith and internal discipline which need not be raised in this context—is why their vision of an 'alternative society' in England failed so rapidly and why they were content to have it so. If the Church of England has taken a semi-conscious decision to give up trying to be the church of the English people, most Free Churchmen seem to have taken it for granted that their future role must simply be that of being junior partners of the Church of England in anything she does rather than that of trying to offer an alternative. This has been very obvious since the founding of the British Council of Churches and the end of the Second World War. The only Free Church group of whom this is not true is the Quakers, and they have always seen their social role in strictly marginal terms. In the light of this, the decision of the Methodist Church to unite with the Anglican was strictly logical in a way which would not have been true in the nineteenth century. What is there any more which divides them, except odd relics of differing social styles such as the use of fermented wine at Communion? It is significant that those within Methodism who resist union with Anglicanism on present terms are chiefly those of former Primitive Methodist allegiance, among whom the roots of old working-class radicalism lie deepest.

This is not necessarily to imply that acceptance of a role of junior partnership with the Church of England is a bad thing in itself. It may be inevitable and, as we shall see, it could be constructive. What is essential is that it should receive more careful and critical analysis from the Free Churches themselves than it has yet been given. Otherwise, they may fail to learn from past mistakes and failures and find themselves in no position to make the kind of contribution they may still be able to make to the common life of England and of Britain. Very searching questions are raised about the nature of Reformed Protestantism by such analysis. This kind of Protestantism, especially in its most self-conscious form, seems to have a gift for losing its impetus and declining. This is very clearly visible in the most self-conscious of all forms of this kind of Protestantism, that of New England. As Perry Miller has shown so clearly in his great series of studies, *The New England Mind, From Colony to Province* and *Errand into the Wilderness*,[29] the aims of the first founders were not fulfilled, even though the indirect consequences of what they did, and even of their very failure, were enormously significant for the future of America. The situation in old England was, of course, more complicated even from the outset, but a similar progression can be traced in the movement of many of the most sensitive and intellectually alert Reformed Protestants from orthodoxy to Unitarianism and the gradual disintegration of their line. Rationalists would naturally be quick to argue that this shows only that they were the most intelligent and independent-minded of churchmen, and therefore were the first to see the illusory character of religion, although the impact of a religious upbringing was so strong that, in most cases, it took more than one generation for the process to work itself out. This is certainly the way in which things seem to happen for many people, but the evidence suggests, all the same, that the matter is nothing like as simple as that. For one thing, it only happened in some cases and, to say the least, those among whom it did not happen were not obviously less intelligent and independent-minded than those among whom it did.[30] There is a good deal of evidence, which cannot be appropriately invoked here, to suggest that the experience of what is so often called 'secularization' today, the mood in which people feel free to organize personal life and communal institutions with no reference to any religious dimension and with a strong conviction of their own ability to cope on the basis of insights they already possess or can readily discover, is one which arises only in the afterglow of a particularly strong religious tradition and one which cannot sustain itself on its own resources for long. Either people's lives sink into insignificance, as seems to be happening to many in great cities today, or else they find a fresh commitment, which may be either to their own tradition in a new form or to quite a different one which seems to make up some of the deficiencies of that which they have rejected. It is the latter which seems to happen most commonly among the strong-minded children of Reformed Protestantism, who have produced many of the more vigorous Catholic converts, Marxists and 'scientific humanists' of the modern world. The more firmly institutionalized expression of ideas and the sense of the importance of maintaining social continuity which finds expression in the attitude of establishments, and pre-eminently of the Anglican Establishment, slows down this process very considerably. If it dampens creativity and hinders reform, it also ensures that the fruits of past achievement are properly gathered, and prevents the over-working of the soil. It has to be admitted that the Church of England has achieved a better 'ecological balance' than the Free Churches in relation to sustaining institutional religious life from one generation to the next. This may, however, be largely due to the fact that it has had, over the generations, steady incursions of new life from the children of the Free Churches. What happens when they are no longer available, we are, perhaps, already beginning to see in the present Anglican decline.

There are three quite specific reasons which help to account for the fact that the Free Churches have never been as effective as they might have hoped in establishing an 'alternative society' in English life.

First, they never fully recovered from the defeat of the Restoration. That may seem to be taking things very far back, but it has affected their whole history. They became a persecuted minority and, although their disabilities were removed, they were removed only slowly and reluctantly and, even after they were, the old Establishment rarely missed an opportunity to slight the Free Churches. Dissenters were ignominiously harried out of public life and inevitably lost something of the sense of wider public responsibility, especially in relation to the use of the power, which they were very rarely allowed to exercise. It is, indeed, to their credit that they retained as much as they did. The quiet urbane dignity of the meeting houses of the eighteenth century, especially those Presbyterian ones which became Unitarian, and the four-square objectivity of the hymns of Isaac Watts, solidly based on biblical faith in the divine government of the world and the covenant between God and Israel, indicate clearly that the public sense was not lost, despite all the disabilities under which Dissenters suffered. The Dissenting Deputies were able to move with skilful self-confidence in public life and, being based on London, were able to take a national view of their position in relation to the established order, with lasting benefit to those who wished to remain English without having to be Anglican.[31] Yet all this was inevitably on a small scale and, until the influence of the Methodist and Evangelical revivals enabled them to broaden their popular appeal, they seemed to be increasingly content with the modest lot. Much of their spiritual energy went into foreign missions rather than into attempts to alter the pattern of English society. By the time of William Blake, the old Dissent had come to seem almost as alien to his vision of an alternative society as did the old Establishment. The truth was that, if eighteenth-century Dissent escaped the aristocratic vices of the period, the aristocracy and its clerical allies took good care to ensure that it should have very few opportunities to cultivate the aristocratic virtues.

Secondly, when, as the nineteenth century developed, scope for more vigorous social and political activity came, it was natural that it should express itself more on the local than on the national level, especially as growing power brought growing Anglican hostility. It was in the new cities and towns of industrial England that the Nonconformists, whether old Dissenters or Methodists, were strongest. As we have seen, their impact on the life of these cities was very considerable and, although their direct influence has largely passed away, they have left an imprint on the style and outlook of the public life of these places which is still discernible. Their influence on smaller communities was even greater, although it has not received the same amount of attention from historians, and has maintained its continuity better, as anyone who visits a place like Darwen or Batley or Saltaire, or, for that matter, Trowbridge or Yeovil or Camborne, can readily discover. Yet even at its best, this vision was too prosaic and domestic, discoloured, as we have seen, in the earlier period by the quasi-individualistic 'voluntarism' of the small manufacturing class and, in the later period, by the sentimental populism of the expanding suburbanized lower-middle class. It is a matter for great regret that that enlargement of the imagination and deepening of the religious sense which Romanticism produced in England and which stimulated Coleridge and Newman inspired no first-class mind to express a vision of an alternative society on terms which could have harnessed the seriousness of Evangelicalism and made fresh links with the seventeenth century at its best. Shelley was an eccentric aristocrat who died too young and Blake's approach was too aesthetic. He was too much in love with his own vision, while his artist's aversion for the realities of power has ensured both that his influence has been slight and that his appeal to unsettled imaginative people has been persistent. If Robert Owen had had a first-class Calvinistic theologian as a friend and both could have gone on a walking tour with Coleridge, or even if the other of the Wesley brothers had been a political pamphleteer and social reformer rather than a hymn writer, something might have happened, but it was not to be.

As it was, when their sheer economic power and the weight of popular support behind them finally brought the Nonconformists back on to the national scene, they were in a poor condition to take advantage of their opportunities. For the most part, they had lost theological depth, and with it the independence of imagination which enables people to stand outside themselves and have something fresh to say both to their own children and to society around them. Dissent had been forced to become an 'interest' as it became politicized, and what self-criticism there was expressed itself more in theological doubts and reductionist essays in restatement than in the re-affirmation of a living tradition in a new situation. Having achieved most of the goals it had set itself in the Liberal administration of 1906–10, it found that it lacked the insight to see further ahead. Its impetus had already diminished when the First World War threw all the elements of English life into disarray.

This, however, is not the whole story. The Dissenting Interest disintegrated after 1918 and political Nonconformity virtually ceased to exist. Yet members of Nonconformist, now more commonly and perhaps more accurately called Free, Churches have, paradoxically, been more prominent in politics and public affairs than they were before, and this has been especially true since 1945. It may be that when Dissent ceased to be a conscious 'Interest', they were released from a partisan loyalty for more disinterested service in the community. The Free Churches, however, have come to have such a minority consciousness that they have made little of this fact, and many of them probably are not even aware of it, more than half-believing themselves the secularist propaganda which says that Christians count for little in communal life today. Yet in the late 1960s, the heyday of the 'swinging sixties', the Prime Minister (and incidentally the Vice-President of the USA), several leading cabinet ministers and the heads of a surprisingly large number of national boards and departments of state were either themselves active and committed Congregationalists of a good deal more than conventional loyalty or were brought up in families of strong Congregational conviction. The proportion of Congregationalists in these positions may have been unusually high, perhaps fortuitously, but the record of members of other Free Church denominations was not markedly different.

What has to be admitted, however, is that few of them have a very clearly-defined vision of England which is different from that of other liberally-minded people in public life, whether they be Anglican or Roman Catholic or nothing very much. It also has to be confessed that they have received precious little help from most of their pastors in reaching one. Such people do their upbringing credit in many ways, but perhaps only a few of them would care to claim that they were consciously carrying on a particular religio-political tradition whose distinctive characteristics as over against others they would be able to define.

All the same, what they have done in changing the character of English public life should not be underestimated. They have succeeded in resisting many of those seductive wiles with which the Conservative Establishment draws the sting of potential opposition. They have rejected the 'aristocratic embrace', which is offered in British life not as a piece of deliberate calculation but as an almost instinctive reaction, which makes it the more attractive and effective. Like Charles II, the old English Establishment has resolved never to go on its travels again, and it does everything in its considerable power to assure any who emerge as possessing ability and social and political influence that all the prizes of membership of their charmed circle are open to them if only they will bow down and worship it, or at least show a decent respect for its leadership and time-honoured patterns of precedence. This it achieved triumphantly in Victorian times, although there were moments such as 1906 when, like the Battle of Waterloo, it was a damned close-run thing. In the end, the vast majority of powerful Victorians were made to see that nothing was more desirable than to end up like that Midland industrialist of Nonconformist stock, honest Stanley Baldwin, voting Conservative and reading the lessons in the parish church like a proper country gentleman. Even today, with two world wars and the second industrial revolution and several Labour governments behind us, and with so many people in the communications industry making such a good thing about mocking those in established positions that they have almost become an establishment in their own right, all the acids of modernity and all the weapons of crusading rationalism seem powerless against them. The deftness shown by the presumptive Charles III in mollifying the potentially hostile natives in his progress through Wales after the ill-advised escapade of his investiture demonstrated that the hand of the Establishment has not lost its cunning and that, barring mishaps, it will be at least another generation or two before its leaders have to go on their travels again.

This is a prospect which, at this time of day, a Free Churchman can contemplate with equanimity if not with any particular enthusiasm. This characteristic mark of the English social genius, 'change as much as you like as long as you do not appear to change', is often a constructive and healing way of making room for necessary adjustments while maintaining continuity. Yet the fact remains that its bias is heavily conservative, and it suits the interests of those in established positions of power and prestige so well that those who do not share fully in their view of society cannot be too easy about it. It blurs too many issues whose outlines ought to be sharpened, and it allows too many undeserving characters to get away, if rarely with murder, too often with petty larceny. The Free Churchmen who are in positions of power today successfully resist many of its blandishments. Otherwise, they would no longer be Free Churchmen. Most of them show a sensitive awareness of ordinary people and their needs and desires up and down the country not always shown by their political opponents or by others in positions of public influence. Yet a more determined attitude on their part towards the traditionalism of the old Establishment might be in order at the present time. The British tradition is not to be identified with that of those of Norman descent and their characteristic institutions. The heirs of those who took part in the Putney Debates of 1647 are far too indulgent towards those who keep pretending, at not inconsiderable public expense, that it is. For example, the role of the House of Lords and the grossly over-loaded honours system have been slightly modified by successive Labour governments. What is surprising, however, is how little has been done to them. It is, no doubt, all to the good that even Labour governments should accept the wisdom of the inevitability of gradualness, but there is reason in everything. When it comes to the point, the literary and intellectual establishments, for all the radical noises they love to make, will nearly always gratefully accept any prizes offered to them.[32] Only those who have a well-defined set of values and order of priorities derived from another source can accept power and responsibility in society and yet extricate themselves from the aristocratic embrace. It would be wonderful if they were able to do so with a grace equal to that which it is frequently offered, but they bear too many of the scars of former deprivations to do that easily. What they can do is to maintain their own independence with the simplicity and directness of their fathers and show a quiet firmness, when they have an opportunity, in doing their part to make the public life of Britain look like that of a democracy in which all have equal consideration and not like the quasi-medieval charade it still so often appears to be.

Whether the Free Churches have enough conviction about their own independent standing-ground to be of any more help to their members in this matter is doubtful. Sometimes they give the impression of being more royalist than the king in their deference to the trappings of establishment. This is the more regrettable because the marked revival of theology and of reinterpretation of their own tradition which has taken place among Free Churchmen over the last thirty or forty years, through the work of Nathaniel Micklem, John Whale, Bernard Manning, Gordon Rupp, Ernest Payne and others, have made them see what resources they have, especially from the seventeenth century, for speaking constructively about English society on the basis of their own history. This theological revival does not, however, seem to have had much direct effect on more than a very few church members. It has certainly done little to encourage them in thinking in specific terms about their distinctive social and cultural task in England, or in Britain as a whole. In all the long discussions which went on between the Church of England and Methodism, very little appears to have been said about the effect on the common life of England that the marriage of these two very different strains would have. It is true, and on its own level very significant, that what unites all the old main-line churches in England is now more important than what divides them, but if reunion is not to mean merging in one uninterestingly uniform mass or, as is more likely if it happens in this way, the absorption of the Free Churches into a diluted form of Anglicanism, it is essential that that which is most distinctive of each tradition at its best should be brought into the union. Creative reunion is a time for the refurbishing and not the blurring of one's ideals, social and cultural as well as religious. It should make each party to the union more, and not less, conscious of its responsibility to what is distinctive in its own heritage in the new context.

The Free Churches have been suffering a steady numerical decline over the last two or three generations. Very few people are alive and active today who can remember the bouncing self-confidence of their life before the First World War, and it may well be that they are so conditioned to a minor social role and to that cosy mediocrity of outlook which goes with it that they can no longer summon up enough vitality to contemplate anything different except that of falling wearily into the arms of the waiting Establishment. Yet there is enough evidence on the other side to suggest that this need not necessarily be so. It is the Anglicans, not the Methodists, who failed to agree to union, and the Congregationalists and Presbyterians have managed it. Free Church ministers may lack the afflatus they had sixty years ago, but they sound a much less uncertain note than many of them did in the heyday of modernism in the twenties, and they often show evidence of a determined and soberly realistic approach to their task of slowly rebuilding their churches from the bottom upwards. Few of the humane and compassionate agencies of society, whether it be bodies like Christian Aid and Oxfam or the more mundane and essential parts of the social, hospital and educational services, could do without the Free Church people on their staff. Like other churches, but perhaps more than most, Free Churches are much weaker than they were, but are far from being at death's door. What they need is an enlargement of the imagination which enables them to see afresh what, given their history and connections, their distinctive function in the future common life of Britain should be.

4 *Roman Catholicism and England*

The emergence of Roman Catholicism as a substantial and *accepted* part of English life is, in modern times, a very recent phenomenon. The ground was being prepared for it much earlier, but it was not until after the Second World War that it became manifest. So far, it has not had much time or opportunity to define itself in distinctively English terms. Educated Roman Catholics have always had a deep interest in cultural questions. This was clearly reflected before and during the war in the pages of the *Dublin Review* and the writings of Christopher Dawson and, under the leadership of the very English Cardinal Hinsley, 'The Sword of the Spirit' movement during the war did a great deal to bring thoughtful Roman Catholics into the midst of the English social debate, but it is probably fair to say that, until quite recently, Catholicism in England as a social and cultural force has been dominated by the outlook and attitudes of immigrant groups. Of these, overwhelmingly the largest and most articulate have been the Irish, particularly the Irish of a few large cities where they were numerous enough to be politically significant, of which Liverpool was the chief. These groups, and especially the Irish, have been more interested in the land which they left behind them than in the land in which they now dwell. This is particularly true on the level of their social ideals. When they have been involved in English politics, it has been chiefly to further the interests of their own groups. Here the safeguarding and furthering of Catholic educational policy has obviously been of supreme importance. In international affairs, they have supported Irish interests and, less vociferously, those of other Catholic countries, especially those engaged in resisting Communism. Yet where these interests have not clashed, the traditional Catholic attitude of deference to the ruling powers has made them very emphatic in asserting their patriotism. A similar attitude is discernible in the USA.

Catholics of different origin, numerically infinitely fewer but socially more influential, have certainly been no less conservative. The old Catholic aristocracy is, traditionally, one of the most conservative groups in the country, and someone like the late Duke of Norfolk often gave the impression of being more part of the Establishment than the Royal Family themselves. Many educated Catholics became Roman Catholics because they believed Rome to be a more reliable custodian of traditional values than the Church of England which, in their view, has always been too ready to adapt its teaching to the prevailing mood in order to curry popular favour. A man like G. K. Chesterton, in his slapdash romantic way, may have had a sense of identification with the distinctive common life of London, with the man on the Clapham omnibus, but he was a Catholic only in the last fourteen years of his life. A more characteristic Catholic writer of his generation, Hilaire Belloc, apart perhaps from *The Bad Child's Book of Beasts* written in his youth, seemed to inhabit a world of the romantic imagination as far removed from modern Britain as possible.

The change which has overtaken the situation today is astonishing. The Church claims, on what is certainly an extremely broad definition of membership, that nearly one person in seven in Britain is a Catholic. The Irish Catholic community is much more widely dispersed through the whole community than it was a generation ago, so that the ghetto-like Irish parish is no longer such a marked feature of the Catholic landscape as it used to be.[33] The presence of sizeable Catholic refugee groups, among whom the Poles stand out, has modified the predominantly Irish nature of the Church in Britain. The number of mixed marriages with people of English descent has done the same. Catholic public schools and the growth in the number of educated converts over the last generation has increased the size of the Catholic upper-middle-class population, whose presence is now quite marked in the professions and in the armed forces. Above all, the spectacular increase in the number of Catholics who have received or are receiving higher education in recent years is sharply altering the social compositions and outlook of the Catholic community. The spreading of the ecumenical movement like wildfire among Catholics, especially but by no means exclusively among those who are highly educated, and the transformation in personal relationships between Catholic priests and their Anglican and Free Church counterparts are bound to have implications so far-reaching that it is impossible at present to assess them.

It is this new relationship to other churches, together with the growth of a much more broadly-based educated Catholic community, which make the change so important. Catholic intellectuals have been a feature, if a marginal one, of English life for a couple of generations or more, but the presence of a large number of educated young Catholics who are of working- or lower-middle-class background and who belong unself-consciously to the ordinary life of England with little sense of being a persecuted minority is a new factor in our cultural situation. Their position is not unlike that of members of the Free Churches at the turn of the century, and it is not surprising that some of them should display similar attitudes.

One of these is that the intellectually self-conscious among them should be more interested in criticizing than in restating their own tradition and that they should be eager to ally themselves with 'radical' social movements. This comes out in the activities of the group who used to publish *Slant*, the now defunct periodical of Catholic radicalism, who proclaim their affinity with the New Left on the one hand and the Leavisite literary tradition on the other. Whatever may ultimately emerge from this, it is hard for an outsider to believe that the characteristic Catholic contribution to English self-definition can be along these lines. Incredible things may have happened to Catholicism in the last few years, but the fact remains that if anyone were seriously interested in reaching Moscow or Peking or Havana in the foreseeable future, this is hardly where he should choose to start from. Fruitful co-operation between Catholics and Marxists may be possible in Brazil, or in Catalonia, but, given the nature of the English hierarchy and given even more the increasing bourgeois prosperity of the English

Catholic population, it is hard to see how any Catholic radicalism, still less any Catholic revolution, could ever get beyond the pages of a little magazine, except temporarily among the Irish on a dockside or a building site. It would be a pity if the refreshing social interest of this group were to expend itself simply in making rhetorical gestures.

Fortunately, there are signs that a revived English Catholicism has plenty of cultural options before it other than those of the extreme right and the extreme left. There is a strong Catholic element in the Labour Party, Professor Michael Fogarty is among the most original of British thinkers about economic and social life, and such Catholic publicists as William Rees-Mogg and Norman St John-Stevas are perceptive interpreters of the conservative tradition in English life. The Jesuit periodical *The Month* is the spokesman of an intelligent Catholic liberalism, and there is enough theological depth and generosity of insight among Catholic 'radicals' themselves to make it probable that they will not be content for long with revolutionary rhetoric. Anyway, it is devoutly to be hoped that this is so, because Catholicism as it is developing has unquestionably a very important part to play in the future matter of England and still more of Britain. The Catholic community is an obvious bridge between the people of England and those of Ireland. And while the strength of the links between Rome and Anglicanism can be exaggerated, since Romans find Anglican claims to catholicity embarrassing and Anglicans find the papal claims and traditional Roman styles profoundly un-English, it is obviously true that, on some levels, Romans and Anglicans share assumptions which they do not have in common either with the Free Churches or the Church of Scotland. Now that we belong to the European Economic Community, English Catholics, with their international and continental links and with their European cast of mind, should be of great assistance in interpreting English attitudes in a European context. A liberalized Catholicism, which retains its theological vitality but which is also sympathetic to its working-class, Scottish and Irish connections and is free from the mannered eccentricity which has limited its conservative intellectual contributions in the past, could be a fresh and creative influence in the future life of Britain. Although the Catholic community is now such an important part of the social and religious life of Britain, it is difficult for an outsider to say more about the form which this influence might take. What is essential, and what seems to be happening, is that the Catholic community should be actively involved in the discussion of the future of England and of Britain and of the churches in relation to that future.

5 *Other religious groups in England*

In such a well-established and conservative society as that of Britain, where we are all expert at the game of ignoring whatever does not fit in with our preconceptions, it is only too easy to think of religious life exclusively in terms of the activities of the familiar large institutions which have long been a part of the public scene. The truth is that there are numerous small and unobtrusive religious sects in Britain, and some, like the Jehovah's Witnesses and the Christian Scientists, which are fairly sizeable communities. Those English people who are apt to speak in superior terms of the proliferation of sects in the USA, would be disconcerted to find how many of those same sects exist in our own towns and cities. Few of these sects may have the kind of self-consciousness which makes them interested in making a direct contribution to the kind of issues discussed in this book, but they themselves represent cultural facts which have to be taken into account by those who are interested in these issues. If, for example, large numbers of ordinary English people join American sects like the Jehovah's Witnesses, whose tenets and style of life represent a sustained protest against many aspects of life in the modern world, and not least against nationalism, that may be a pointer to the extent of the alienation from the dominant ideals of our society which exists among people who otherwise might be inarticulate. Likewise, if elderly and conservative people in the most conservative neighbourhoods of the country were to become British Israelites in large numbers, who take virtually the opposite direction from the Jehovah's Witnesses while moving in what might be called the same universe of discourse, that, in its turn, would say something about the

extent to which naively pious people feel betrayed by the representatives of the institutions in which they have traditionally put
their trust about the ideals for British life which they have always
cherished.

The size of such groups in our midst is sufficiently large to be a
warning that such alienation and frustration exist and that religious
and quasi-religious longings can take very curious forms when they
are bound up with cultural attitudes and a concern for the well-
being of society. The unexpected religious gyrations of some young
people in recent years have underlined the same truth in a different
context, although it should not be overlooked that not a few young
people find their way into the Jehovah's Witnesses and other
American sects as well as into Eastern cults. It is undoubtedly
significant for present-day society that members of the 'underground' have come up into the daylight again. The 'underground'
represents the attitudes of those who explore options about human
life, whether in relation to sexual behaviour, personal appearance,
political organizations or to ways of reaching knowledge, which
have been rejected and pushed underground in the past, either
by consensus or deliberate acts of suppression. Its reappearance is
always the sign that a sufficient number of the members of a
community have so lost confidence in the inherited values of that
society as to make them want to challenge their dominance. It is a
sign also of the need to restate and defend those values or modify
them in the light of fresh insight. It could, therefore, herald a new
era of creative development, although in itself it is not necessarily
creative. To bring the inhabitants of the 'underground' into the
daylight may serve only to throw into relief how wise our forefathers were to reject them and convince us in our turn that it is
best to thrust what they stand for back where it belongs. This is
certain to be true of those who love being part of the underground
for its own sake, who are creatures who love the night because
their works are evil. Yet this should not allow those who dwell in
what they believe to be the daylight to ignore the fact that the
re-emergence of the underground is always a sign that there is
something wrong, and that it also carries with it the possibility that
something new and better is being born.

In all honesty, it is very hard to see any sign of where this possibility shows signs of being actualized. It is true that any new thing which is genuinely new is bound to be small at its beginnings and therefore easily overlooked. In these days also, the media of communication are so feverishly anxious to discover any novelty and then to give it the maximum exposure before making room for the next novelty that it is probably a mark of any genuine new development that it is careful to eschew all publicity. We may continue to hope, therefore, that something may be happening which is not yet visible and be content to await its appearance in its own good time. Meanwhile, there is no alternative to looking over the rest of the familiar field to see if anyone else has anything to offer.

That something new might emerge out of the Society of Friends has always seemed a possibility. They stand a little apart from the main body of the Free Churches and they not only contain a large number of highly educated and socially effective people but still have the power of attracting such from outside, in a way in which most other Free Churches conspicuously fail to do. They are, as ever, indefatigably diligent in good works, and what was said about the social role of the larger Free Churches earlier applies even more forcibly to the Society of Friends. One of their most admirable qualities is their quietness, and what they have been trying to do for peace in behind-the-scenes activity for reconciliation between East and West will probably not be fully known in our time. Yet, for all their virtues, modern Quakers in England seem as deficient as anyone else in energy and original ideas. Many of the best British architects are Quakers, yet Quakers today seem to lack a distinctive vision of what 'a pure and peaceable kingdom' might mean in visual terms in modern England, or even to possess enough energy to produce an up-dated version of the kind of practical idealism which inspired the creation of Bournville. This is a pity when so much community re-building has to be done and when it is obvious that we have not yet solved the problem of how to make a success of new towns and communal redevelopment.

The story of the Salvation Army is disappointing. No organization has a finer record of good works and it still maintains a remarkable number of activities which are very close to the ground of basic human needs. But the modern Army underlines the sad truth that even a tradition of service provides no substitute for the astringent preservative quality of self-criticism. Military styles and disciplines may not be inappropriate for a religious organization conducting a short-term campaign. They could not be worse for an old-established religious group needing to reform and renew itself, as all must if they are to continue to possess vitality. Recent attempts to put a top-dressing of trans-Atlantic public relations gimmickry upon the Army's activities are particularly regrettable. The Salvation Army has too fine a history and plays too significant a part in the network of social services and has too many admirable people involved in its work, to allow itself to move in this direction. More than most bodies, it would seem to stand to benefit from participation in an open conversation about the future of churches as well as social service organizations in British life, but whether it now has too large a vested interest in its own traditions and distinctive activities for this to happen remains to be seen.

What is likely to happen to the British Jewish community is, again, a very difficult matter of speculation, and no outsider dare make any but the most tentative of observations. For the most part, Jewish people in England have been as loyal as they have been diligent, content either to be assimilated into the wider culture and to share many of its ideals or to maintain quietly their own firm identity as members of a sub-culture within the framework of the more general culture in which, with the exception of its overt Christian observances, they have been relatively at ease. The emergence of the state of Israel as an external focus of political loyalty has obviously complicated the situation. Whatever may happen as a result of this, there can be no question that for Jewish people to withdraw from full participation in the life of England because of their preoccupation with the matter of Israel would be a great impoverishment of English life. A periodical like the excellent American *Commentary* would perform an extremely valuable function in British life today, and perhaps it is permissible to say that Jewish philanthropists might employ their money better in endowing such a venture than in putting up elaborate new buildings for the use of Gentiles in already over-privileged ancient universities. The closely-knit social organization, the political liberalism and the dispassionate observation of others, if not always of themselves, of the highly intelligent Jewish community is a valuable ingredient in the British social mixture. The big question may be whether there is enough distinctively religious vitality in modern Judaism to provide it in sufficient measure.

History suggests that new life is more likely to come from the emergence of new social groups, previously unformed or denied an outlet, into the fuller life of society than from the renewal of old ones. In this case, the immigrant groups who have recently come to settle in Britain would be the place to look. Of these, perhaps the West Indians, who have a strong sense of British identity and who often bring their own distinctive forms of Pentecostalism with them, are the most promising, not least because they are the group most conscious of tension in dealing with their white neighbours. Another generation has to pass, however, before anyone can begin to see whether any new light is likely to come from this or any similar quarter. It has to be remembered also that, despite the tension already mentioned, the processes of assimilation to the ordinary life of society, through education and the standardization of the media of communication, now run so smoothly that any leadership has to be very strong to enable people to have a vision of society and their role in trying to bring it into being which is significantly different from that of their neighbours. This has long been true of native English people of working-class background. The possibility of a revolution of the 'workers' is largely a myth of alienated children of the professional classes. The workers want the same things as most members of the 'middle classes', and when they have them they develop similar attitudes, often enough in cruder and more self-centred forms. This is why what the more educated members of English society want and how they set about obtaining it is so important for the whole community. Whether women, many of whom see themselves very clearly today as members of a still imperfectly emancipated group, might generate new cultural vitality, is a possibility which must not be left out of account, but women themselves will have to indicate the directions which this might take.

It is fashionable at present among some self-conscious people to say the Western tradition is bankrupt and that the inherited values of England, those of her religion and patriotic loyalty and family life, must be repudiated. This carries with it a new interest (it can hardly be called much more than that at present) in Eastern religion, notably some forms of Buddhism, and in the view of the world associated with it. One could not look to such an attitude for the renewal of the English vision, since part of its point would be to deny the validity of such a vision. Without forgetting that new movements always have small beginnings, the character of this interest is such as to make inescapable a certain scepticism as to whether anything significant will arise directly from it. One of the puzzling things about the Western world, which may be related to the heavy burden of self-consciousness which its children have to carry, is that it seems to suffer periodic waves of disenchantment with itself, a disenchantment which embraces its cultural style and its science as well as its religion, so that people feel that they have to look anywhere but into their own heritage for enlightenment. It may well be that there is new light to come to us from the East, or forgotten light to be rediscovered, but Eastern faiths must first be studied in their own terms and the measure of the forces arranged against them in the Western world must be taken.[34] Past experience with similar moods, as in New England at the end of the nineteenth century, suggests that these efforts to appropriate the insight of other cultures lack the depth, intensity and infectious power to have much influence on reshaping the life of a society so dynamic as ours. Any alternative faith for England and the Western world (and this holds equally for any attempted radical restatement of the inherited Christian faith) cannot by-pass but must go beyond all that we have learnt from the Middle Ages and the Renaissance, the Reformation, the Enlightenment and the scientific revolution, and must also show that it has the strength either to tame or to destroy the monsters unleashed by modern technology.

NOTES

1. Dietrich Bonhoeffer, *Letters and Papers from Prison: The Enlarged Edition*, SCM Press 1971, pp. 6f. See also the brief discussion of his thought from this point of view in Heinrich Ott, *Reality and Faith*, Lutterworth Press 1971, pp. 297–9.

2. *Church and State*, Church Information Office 1970.

3. A. N. Whitehead, *Essays in Science and Philosophy*, Greenwood Press, New York 1968, p. 21. For Whitehead, Tait was the last of the line of great ecclesiastics for whom 'the church was the nation rising to the height of its civilization'. 'Since his time', he added, 'English ecclesiastical policy has been directed to organizing the Anglican Church as a special group within the nation'.

4. D. M. Paton (ed.), *Essays in Anglican Self-Criticism*, SCM Press 1958.

5. The Australian church, under the inspiration of Bishop Burgmann, has done work along these lines but largely in terms of the Australian situation itself. The whole subject of the relation of distinctively British parts of the Commonwealth like Australia, New Zealand and most of Canada, to British identity, is one that demands further examination.

6. It is surprising that the prayer book of the Protestant Episcopal Church of the USA has remained so very much like that of its English and Scottish counterparts, with the only striking modification that of the state prayers. If it had remained an ethnic church, cherishing the folk memory of an exiled national group, this would have been understandable, but it is emphatically American, with many of its leaders not of Anglo-Saxon extraction at all. As long ago as the late thirties, I used to derive mild enjoyment from the discomfiture of my English Anglican fellow-students by asking them whom they considered the most politically influential Anglican layman in the world. Their usual reply was Lord Halifax, at that time the Foreign Secretary and well known as a devoted churchman. They were surprised when I disagreed and said that Franklin Delano Roosevelt and Fiorello la Guardia were stronger candidates. Yet the Protestant Episcopal Church never seems to have taken serious account of the non-English elements in its life, any more than the Church of England has bothered much about the implications of its international associations for its own domestic life.

7. The only independent discussion of the Coronation has been undertaken by two sociologists, one American: Michael Young and Edward Shils, 'The Meaning of the Coronation', *Sociological Review*, December 1953.

8. E. C. Ratcliffe, *The Coronation Service*, Cambridge University Press 1953.

9. Apart from anything else, as far as the Coronation service itself is concerned, there are elements of the ridiculous in the present situation

which should not be allowed to perpetuate themselves. They may only be visible to a small circle of the knowledgeable, but they are none the less inappropriate for that. It has already been freely acknowledged that there are many aspects of the Coronation service which fill a non-Anglican with awestruck admiration, in particular the combination of simplicity and directness with formality and the ability to make changes which enrich rather than detract from the sense of continuity. The contribution of Ralph Vaughan Williams to the last two Coronations is an excellent example of the latter point. But quite apart from the large matters already dealt with, there is some very dubious business from any Christian viewpoint in relation to the 'honours of England' and, in particular, there is an aspect of the service, entirely within the church's control, which no intelligent student of the Old Testament can observe without an ironical smile. Everyone admires the splendid Handel Coronation anthems, sung with such superb afflatus by the Abbey choir at the last Coronation and frequently played over since. Very few appear to have pondered on the words in their context of a ruthless power struggle in II Kings, where the elements of pride and pomposity in the regal pretensions of Solomon are underlined and where Zadok the priest is full of deep misgivings about the whole operation and performs his function with obvious hesitations and qualifications. Responsible churchmen surely owe it to their monarch and their country to bring out not so much the divinity as the ambivalence which doth hedge a king in biblical understanding rather than to permit the singing of a musical setting of these words produced by the eighteenth century at its most complacent, even if also at its most accomplished. To allow a solemn act in which vast numbers of people participate in good faith, including many of those directly involved, to have even the hint of a pretentious charade is not a proper exercise of their office on the part of the churchmen with a trained sense of history.

10. Ian Henderson, *Power without Glory*, Hodder 1967.

11. Thomas Arnold, quoted in Stanley's *Arnold*, II, 337 and cited by C. R. Sanders, *Coleridge and the Broad Church Movement*, Duke University Press 1942, p. 115.

12. Nor is it always true that it is only the socially privileged and their dependents who are Anglican. What was striking about that same post-war period was the extent to which the Parish Communion and, in particular, the 'Parish and People' movements, through which the modest Anglican revival of the time found its chief expression, emancipated themselves from traditional class-consciousness. Much of their support came from people who, a generation before, would have been more at home in one of the liberal Free Churches.

13. See F. D. Maurice, *The Kingdom of Christ* II, SCM Press 1958, and the succeeding chapter.

14. David Newsome, *Godliness and Good Learning: Studies in a Victorian Ideal*, John Murray 1961.

15. Evidence of this is the number of their ministers interested in social issues who christened their children 'Kingsley'.

16. Most of his books were reissued by the Independent Press in London in the years immediately after the Second World War.

17. See William Temple, *What Christians Stand for in the Secular World*, SCM Press 1944.

18. A usefully critical note, however, is struck by H. Cunliffe-Jones, 'A New Assessment of F. D. Maurice's *The Kingdom of Christ*', *Church Quarterly* IV, 1, July 1971, pp. 38ff.

19. Simon Raven, *The English Gentleman*, Blond 1961, p. 17.

20. Denis Brogan, *The English People*, Hamish Hamilton 1943.

21. See the self-critical observations along these lines in Christopher Driver, *The Disarmers*, Hodder 1964, and the little known but scintillating book by H. F. Lovell Cocks, *The Nonconformist Conscience*, Independent Press 1942.

22. See Peter H. Hennock, *Fit and Proper Persons*, Edward Arnold, 1973.

23. Edward Thompson, *The Making of the British Working Class*, Gollancz 1963.

24. See David Martin's article 'The Unknown Gods of the English', *The Religious and the Secular*, Routledge 1969, pp. 111f.

25. George Elder Davie, *The Democratic Intellect*, Edinburgh University Press 1961.

26. Richard Hofstadter, *Anti-Intellectualism in American Life*, Cape 1964.

27. Christopher Hill, *Puritanism and Revolution*, Secker & Warburg 1958, preface, p. vii.

28. Peter Hennock, *Fit and Proper Persons*, Part II, chs. 1, 6, 7.

29. All published by Harvard University Press. For a more qualified but not basically different analysis see Larzer Ziff, *Puritanism in America*, Oxford University Press 1973.

30. Is there a point of fully 'emancipated' enlightened rationalism which anyone ever reaches, where he is free from the kind of constraint upon him out of which a fresh religious or quasi-religious commitment has to arise if he is to do anything worth-while and satisfying with his life?

31. See B. L. Manning and Ormerod Greenwood, *The Dissenting Deputies*, Cambridge University Press 1957.

32. Thus the public scene is adorned by such unexpected figures of knightly chivalry as Sir Alfred Ayer and such majestic pillars of the house of peers as the Lady Wootton of Abinger.

33. See C. K. Ward, *Priest and People*, Liverpool University Press 1961.

34. David L. Edwards, *Religion and Change*, Hodder 1969, ch. 5, analyses very carefully some of the factors involved in such an enterprise.

V

THE COMMUNITY OF BRITAIN

1   *The internal relations of the British*

If those who wish to maintain the distinctive English, Scottish and Welsh heritages in the modern world are to have any hope of success, they must see each other as allies rather than as enemies. Their heritages may differ but their attitudes towards them are similar. What they cherish most are either qualities they have in common or those which complement each other, and the problems they face are virtually the same. The Scots and the Welsh may agree that this is so in relation to each other but will say that this is not so in relation to the English. There are, and always have been, qualifying factors in the situation because of English size and dominance, but what is significant about the present time is that the need to make these qualifications is becoming steadily less pronounced. We all find ourselves together in the same boat. Modern technology, and the rising standard of living which it brings, forces upon all alike the need for concentration of population, standardization of goods and centralization of control. The price of prosperity is the apparent loss of distinctive identity.

The extent to which this affects everyone is concealed both because, as usual, it is the English, or at least those who live in England, who seem to derive most benefit from this process and because the English, with their strong inherited majority consciousness, appear to have noticed it least. The most Scots parts of Scotland, at least until the very recent discovery of North Sea oil, and the most Welsh parts of Wales are on the margin of the modern world, but South-East England is still close to its centre. This will becomes even more true now that Britain has joined the European Community. What is forgotten, however, is that the price which the South-East has to pay, is, if anything, even higher than anything which Scotland or Wales have to face. The South-East of England is increasingly becoming an international community. This is at its most obvious in central London, but it is true with varying degrees of intensity throughout, as the residents of East Kent can testify with feeling as the juggernauts rumble by. The impact of this on the English is less vivid only because of this majority consciousness already mentioned. They are more ready than the Scots and the Welsh, especially the latter, to believe that this is a situation which they can use to their own advantage. They are also adept at creating fictions which enable them to ignore unpalatable facts and save face. From the monarchy downwards, the English have an incomparable gift for practising the gentle semideceptions with which the Misses Jenkyns in Cranford contrived to maintain their status as prosperous gentlefolk, even though they knew and their friends knew and they knew that their friends knew that things were not really quite so. It is only recently that some English people who have long since bought their suits at Burtons and their shirts at Marks and Spencer stopped speaking of 'my tailor' and 'my shirt-maker', and it will take them much longer to admit not only that Britannia no longer rules the waves but that she is only partially mistress in her own house. There may well be wisdom in this attitude because it maintains the maximum degree of continuity, prevents the English from having a chip on their shoulder and sometimes convinces others as well as themselves that they still have power, but it does not alter the facts.

Thus, it is well known that increasingly large and important parts of British industry are owned by American firms, and Americans do not discriminate much between one part of Britain and another. A worker at Ford's in Dagenham or Chrysler's in Coventry is even more at the mercy of a decision taken across the Atlantic than one in the Upper Clyde shipyards or at the Hoover factory in Merthyr. Even if the control of a firm remains in British hands, the interests of a particular place or region are rarely consulted. Executives and their wives may prefer, other things being equal, to live in or near London, but not much weight is given to such considerations when major decisions are involved. The psychological effect of having one's firm taken over by another is not so very different whether the decision to do so is taken in Glasgow or London or Brussels or New York.

Nor is the situation so very different in relation to less flexible commodities and more permanent resources. The Welsh become indignant, often with reason, at having their valleys flooded in order to provide water for English industrial cities. The inhabitants of the Lake District and the Yorkshire Dales become no less indignant, and are only slightly mollified by the thought that Manchester and Bradford are in England. To a dalesman, these cities are almost as alien as Liverpool is to an inhabitant of Bala. Likewise with the other contentious matter of forestry plantations. Hill farmers feel much the same about it wherever they are, and any differences of attitude which may exist between, say, mid-Wales and the Scottish Border country are due to the different systems of sheep farming, not to any differences of nationality.

The same holds also over the identity problems of educational institutions. Welsh Nationalists are incensed at the threat posed by the invasion of English students to the integrity of what they regard as distinctively Welsh institutions, the university colleges of Aberystwyth and Bangor. This is a real threat, and to know how to deal with it, especially in such small-scale institutions, requires a good deal of thought and the balancing of a variety of important considerations, but the situation is not helped if it is assumed that this is no more than another English plot to destroy Welsh identity. English universities, no less, are being internationalized, especially by the flood of American students beating with increasing force upon these shores. The authorities of the London School of Economics can speak with as much feeling as the Welsh department at Aberystwyth about the problems of identity which this raises.[1]

Even on the contentious matters of television and the press, there are some factors in the situation which are frequently over-looked. It is true that London dominates these, but it is London as a national and international centre which dominates them, not London as the centre of its own region. In fact, any man of Essex or Kent or Sussex concerned with the identity of his own county, which is a quite recognizable thing, can reasonably claim to be discriminated against, since his local activities, like those of the vast tracts of unfashionable London, are largely ignored. In Wales it is always agreeable to hear on the radio the results of football matches played in the infinitely minor Mid-Wales League, but quite important amateur games played in South-Eastern England are never mentioned. The development of local radio is beginning to make a difference, but it has a long way to go.

These points are not made in order to stop the Scots or the Welsh, or for that matter Cornishmen or Yorkshiremen, from complaining, but simply to underline the fact that these problems are common problems, and that they are so serious that they will not be solved unless we co-operate with each other in meeting them.[2] The benefits brought by modern technology are desirable to nearly everyone but, as is becoming clear on many levels today, they are brought at the sacrifice of other good things and they have to be looked at more carefully to see whether the price for them is worth paying. They threaten, and often destroy, precious assets of civilization which are neither quantifiable nor easily replaceable. The nature of modern technology makes it look for the easiest way of doing things, to take the line of least resistance and to ignore everything which is prepared to get out of its way. It is the duty of those who are the primary custodians of human values to refuse to get out of the way and to demand that those values be taken into account. Politicians and publicists and planners and parsons and teachers all have their part to play in this and, when they refuse to do it, it is useless for them to blame engineers and businessmen for behaving like engineers and businessmen.

In this task the exclusive nationalism, or regionalism, or parochialism which sees one's own problems as unique is a hin-drance and not a help. A larger view has to be taken if human values are genuinely to be served. It is not enough to keep the reservoir out of my valley or the airport away from our village and then to have a service of thanksgiving when we succeed. Someone has to take decisions about the proper use and allocation of water resources and the proper siting of airports, and there must be a careful balancing of interests which has to be done even in deciding who that someone must be. Otherwise, what happens is that the most aggressive pressure group wins a victory and that the weakest and least vociferous, who may have the best case, go to the wall.

It is hard to see why, in our British situation, there need be any special difficulty about this kind of co-operation between those of like mind in the various countries. The difficulties arise largely because most of these people simply have no contact with each other and have had no opportunity for conversation which might show how much they have in common. Certainly, it is hard to see what objection there can be to such co-operation on Christian grounds. We have seen that a Christian attitude towards nationality means both a respectful attitude to national identity and its distinctive forms of expression and also a recognition of their relativity and of the dangers which emerge when that relativity is not admitted. This makes it natural for people to want to co-operate with others of like mind across national boundaries while at the same time being determined to maintain their own identity. The British situation is one in which this kind of co-operation is exceptionally easy, and experience has proved it to be so. Scots and Welsh Nationalists would deny this, but one wonders how hard they have tried and whether they have not had a political interest in exacerbating difficulties. Obviously any kind of international relationship is complex and it requires skill and understanding to adjust separate loyalties to each other, while occasional clashes may be unavoidable. But the more mature a society is, and the more civilized and responsible its members are, the better they become at doing this. After all, every form of government, even the most centralized, recognizes and defines gradations of responsibility. Certain important rights are ceded to local and regional forms of government, and the relation of these to central government becomes a significant aspect of the art of government. If this can be managed even in the areas of the common life most affected by the realities of power, it should be easier to achieve in more informal social and cultural relationships. Once more, this is something which we understand very well in Britain, and this understanding needs to be built up and not torn down.

The one major qualification which has to be made in all this, as is clear from the whole trend of the argument, is over the attitude of the English towards the Scots and the Welsh. Nothing must be allowed to diminish the sense of urgency with which the English need to reconsider their attitude towards the distinctive identities of Scotland and Wales. Yet it is important in a time when fresh adjustments in relationship have to be made not to exaggerate the difficulties nor to disparage, or simply to take for granted as of no significance, the successes. When looking at the situation, it is natural to call attention to the failures because something generally has to be done about them, but to see internal relations in this country only in terms of difficulties is to create a false atmosphere, in which unnecessary obstacles to constructive discussion are raised. Over large areas of life, we do contrive to live happily as a people who are both united and different. Paradoxically, one of the difficulties that the English have in taking problems of Scottish and Welsh identity seriously is that most of the Scots and Welsh people they meet do not look like people with problems, but like people, often successful people, as much at home as they are in the same society.

The elder who gave out the notices, called the *cyhoeddwr* in Welsh, at a Welsh Presbyterian church in London which I used occasionally to attend many years ago to hear the best sermons in London, was a man of fine presence, relaxed, tactful and assured, who was obviously held in high esteem by his fellow members. I once happened to be in a large London department store much patronized by conservative English families, and there, standing in the middle of the crowded ground floor, stood a man of fine presence, relaxed, tactful and assured, obviously in charge and constantly being consulted by staff and public. It took me a little time to recall where I had seen him before and to realize that this was the *cyhoeddwr*. Here was a man who appeared to be completely at home in two widely differing communities, in which he displayed similar qualities and, to all appearances, evoked similar responses. His story is typical of a great multitude. The Welsh have amply demonstrated their ability to run an International as well as a National Eisteddfod. Intelligent Scotsmen and Welshmen find it easy to be good Scotsmen and good Welshmen and at the same time to participate fully in the wider life of Britain. The English, the Scots and the Welsh intermarry freely and, in may cases, the differences of national background are seen as a source of enrichment rather than of weakness to the family. In these days especially, whatever may have been the case in the past, it by no means necessarily follows that the Scottish and the Welsh elements lose out to the English.

In his illuminating book *The Religious Factor*,[3] the American sociologist Gerhard Lenski has shown, through a study of ethnic minority groups in Detroit, chiefly Italian and Polish Roman Catholics, how it is possible for a vigorous sub-culture to survive into the seventh and eighth generation within the context of a great city where the dominant group is of a different stock and style of life. It is true that in the process the sub-culture has inevitably been modified, but so has the dominant culture, and it could be argued that both are the better for the contact. This has happened even in the so-called 'melting-pot' of America, where the social and economic pressures towards 'Americanization' are strong, and there seems to be no reason in the nature of the situation why it should not continue to happen in Britain.

What have to be clearly understood are the attitudes and the context in which this is possible. The minority groups must have a vigorous will to survive and must be present in sufficient numbers to maintain their characteristic institutions, of which their churches are often the most important, and to give each other economic and social support. The context is no less important. There must be a system of representative government which reflects, with reasonable accuracy, the interests of the various groups within the community and which allows for a great deal of social and cultural pluralism over wide areas of life. This, in its turn, is only possible where there is also a large area in which there is substantial agreement about the nature of society. As in all democratic politics, but more than in less mixed communities, there must be a great deal of flexibility and readiness to compromise. It is essential that no serious discrimination exists against minority groups on the ground of their sub-nationality, race or colour, especially in the public service. It means reasonable access for all to the means, chiefly those of education and training, by which power, influence and wealth are achieved, what we love euphemistically to call 'equality of opportunity'. No less important, it also means that the minority should not be so strong, closely-knit, successful and intolerant that the majority feel that their own style of life is threatened by them. This is not simply a matter of the majority calculating that, whatever happens, they will always hold the power. If it were, few majorities could resist the temptation so to discriminate against the minority as to ensure that they could never hope for power. This is what happens in parts of Africa and has been alleged by Catholics to happen in Northern Ireland and it breeds a situation of political instability, poisoned by fear and resentment. It has to be a situation in which the majority are not seriously worried whether members of the minority gain power or not, since they remain confident that the minority also would want to preserve those characteristics of the society which the majority consider essential and that any modifications they might be called upon to make would not be intolerable. By the same token, members of the minority groups need to be able to participate in public life, whether in politics or in staffing the major institutions of society, without feeling that they are betraying the interests of their minority in doing so, or without being held by a substantial section of that minority to be guilty of such a betrayal. The majority and the minority must have sufficient respect for and understanding of each other to be able to work a society together, and to make common cause when their common interests are threatened by an outside power in which neither of them has any confidence.

It is hard to see how anyone can honestly deny that these conditions exist, and have existed for some time, in modern Britain. Of course, as in all societies, they do so imperfectly and with anomalies and injustices which need to be dealt with here and there, but to use the existence of these as an excuse for throwing over what we already have is to make perfectionist demands which cannot possibly be met and which will only clear the ground for something worse than what already exists. This is not to imply that, therefore, all is for the best in the best of all possible worlds in modern Britain. Awareness of the dangerously high level of frustration and indignation among Scots and Welsh people has been one factor in leading to the writing of this book. With our two-party system organized as it is, with English complacency as deep-rooted as it is and with the most vulnerable and most precious parts of Scotland and Wales needing as much intelligent help as they do, a more radical revision of our governmental arrangements than most people in Whitehall are prepared to contemplate at present may well prove to be necessary. This is why the proposals of the Kilbrandon Commission should be given careful attention, more careful attention than the British Parliament, with its constant obsession with economic matters, has yet shown itself prepared to give. All the same, the wrong climate is created for any action along these lines if people deny that Lenski's conditions substantially exist in Britain and, in order to try to prove the contrary, then magnify every unintentional slight or piece of governmental ineptitude to the dimensions of a major crisis.

What is vital is that English people should be made to see that the initiative in trying to keep the general context of British life healthy and in diminishing the present threat to our internal harmony rests with them. It is the Scottish and Welsh sense of identity which feels threatened at present. (The English sense of identity is almost equally threatened but, for the reasons which have already been given, most English people do not see it so clearly.) If the greatest enemy to all the distinctive cultures of these islands is not dominant Englishness but certain tendencies in the modern world to which the English, partly because of their size and prosperity, are no less vulnerable than the other nations, the English must become more aware of this and make some significant gestures of solidarity with the Scots and Welsh in trying to resist the evil effects of these tendencies. Apart from anything else, to the extent to which the English succumb to them, they make it the more difficult for the Scots and the Welsh to resist them just because our economies and ways of life are so inextricably bound up with each other. Even the most liberal and self-critical of English people may find it hard honestly to believe that they have been 'colonialist' in their attitude to the other nations of this island, but they must, at least, accept the fact that many members of these nations have, whether rightly or wrongly, developed some of the attitudes of resentment characteristic of the educated children of colonialist peoples. If the British Empire was built in a fit of absent-mindedness, the United Kingdom could easily, and quite unnecessarily, become the disunited kingdom in the same way. The English have to see what it is always very hard to see, that the main trouble lies not in what they do but in what they take for granted and what they have left undone. Their 'tranquil consciousness of effortless superiority' has largely been knocked out of them in dealing with the USA, Asia and Africa, and will not have much room to express itself in relations with the Common Market countries, but it can still indulge itself in dealings with the Scots and, in particular, the Welsh, their traditional poor relations. They can no longer afford to do so. The English really must be on their guard. If the Scots and Welsh make themselves sufficiently obstreperous, and it is easy for quite small groups of them to do this with all the sophisticated modern techniques for un-neighbourly behaviour, the English will vote them more money. They will continue to let the Welsh have their road signs in their own tongue and, if sufficiently pressed, they will give them a measure of parliamentary devolution to get them out of their hair. What they will not give them is what is essential: time, attention and intelligently serious interest both in their history and in their distinctive future.

This is the more important because many Scots and even more Welsh people are not disposed to act with complete rationality in the present situation. They feel that their very hearths are seriously threatened, and there is an element of desperation in the way in which people defend their homes. The English will also need to remember that if being a part of a vulnerable minority makes one touchy and self-righteous, being a part of a long-established majority makes one complacent and insensitive. The English cannot afford to be like this any longer because it is not as easy as it used to be to export their problems overseas. If it be argued that entering the European Economic Community changes all this, the answer is that, on the contrary, it could make it worse unless there is a change of English attitude. It is the English, and especially the southern English, who are in the best position to benefit from entry. They will be very tempted to say, with that 'common sense' on which they pride themselves, 'Going into Europe means that we must forget all our little local differences, concentrating on what we have in common and all pulling together.' Scots and Welsh people interpret that as meaning, 'Think and act like Englishmen and don't bother us with your problems. Otherwise you will hinder us from making a success of going into Europe, which will work chiefly to our advantage but, if we do well enough, may enable us to spare a few crumbs for you also.' One can only hope that the difficulties which the English are likely to experience in asserting their own identity when facing the powerful Six, who have more in common with each other than any of them have with England, may help to give the English a new understanding of how the Scots and the Welsh feel in dealing with the English.

It will not be enough, however, for the English to acknowledge and pay serious attention to Scottish and Welsh identity, essential as that is before anything else can be done. All of us need a clearer idea of what binds us together, and especially of what binds us together on those levels where we genuinely want to be together. I have said that we need each other and the best of each other, and that much of the best is what is most distinctive of each. But it is equally true that a good deal of that best is to be found in what we have in common, especially when we consider our aspirations rather than our achievements. This is why the effort must be made, difficult as it may be, to restate what the common elements are in our ideals for community life in these islands.

2   The ideal of Britain

If the British way of life is one of balance in tension rather than that of a unified community moving towards a commonly acknowledged goal, any attempt to define the British ideal has to be complex, and subject to many qualifications. It also has to point beyond what has already been realized to possibilities which are not yet fully visible.

One of the complications is that, as we have seen, there are no satisfactory words to describe the two main elements in our life. The most common traditional labels in English terms, 'Cavalier' and 'Roundhead', still have a rough and ready usefulness, but they are increasingly archaic and do not apply directly to the Welsh and the Scots. Yet the two attitudes which have to be held in balanced tension are clear enough and are readily recognizable. The one is that of those who believe that the British understanding of human nature and its relation to society and its institutions has reached a measure of definition and expression sufficiently satisfactory as to be preserved at all costs. It is conservative to the core. It does not resist all change—part of its wisdom lies in its recognition that some changes are inevitable—but it accepts change reluctantly. It considers nothing as more dangerous than the creation of a precedent and is unhappy until it has been able to fit new departures into existing patterns. Those who can do this in such a way as to make a break in continuity invisible to the naked eye are greatly admired.

It is this England, rather than what found expression in St Paul's, which T. S. Eliot, who came out of that part of the English-speaking world which had built itself very consciously on the other element in the British tradition, came to love, the England of his Classicism, Royalism and Anglicanism, and it was with the fervour of a convert that he defended it against any attempt to come to terms with that other element which might threaten its unique quality.[4] Those who hold this view of England are never happy about moving away from the land, which they believe to be the traditional source of its health as well as its wealth. In so far as this attitude has a geographical base, those who hold it are to be found chiefly in the least industrialized parts of Southern England and in the parts of the North, like the Vale of York, most like those of the South. It is these people who feel the Scots and the Welsh to be most alien to them and who react instinctively against ideas which derive from sources outside their own life, especially, as they would say, from over-intellectualized France, over-intense Germany and restless America.

Those who hold the other attitude in British life may be no less convinced that the British bear many of the marks of a chosen people, but they think of their vocation in much more biblical terms. They see themselves as pilgrims, those 'who seek a country', and they are not as convinced as those on the other side that they have already found it. They may believe just as fervently that, in some sense at least, 'those feet in ancient time walked upon England's mountains green', but they see this not so much as a good reason for keeping them as green as possible but rather for not letting their sword sleep in their hand. This attitude found its fullest expression in the Puritanism of the seventeenth century, but its succession can obviously be traced, inevitably qualified in various directions, in Evangelicalism, Methodism and Romanticism, in Victorian Nonconformity and in much modern liberalism and 'progressivism'.[5] Its roots lie very deep in English soil, but it has much stronger affinities with the predominant modern forms of Scottish and Welsh life, not to say American, than the other attitude. It is also more sympathetic to outside influences, especially those which are new and radical, and these in the nineteenth century were generally German.

In discussing the matter of England, it was said that the predominant traditional view of the English, the so-called Cavalier attitude, was that which thought of society as an organism, like a tree, rather than the conscious attempt to give expression to an idea. If they were asked about their ideal for British life, however, most people who hold this view would probably say that it was more adequately thought of in the figure of a family. The biological basis and the concern for continuity remain, but they are given their full human value. For these people, the monarchy has all the majesty attached to dedicated power, but their ideal for the monarchy is that it should behave like the head of the family.[6] The framework and the order of precedence are to be taken for granted, but within them there must be sympathy and mutual consideration. Those who carry responsibility, and who enjoy the privileges which rightly go with it, have obligations to those who depend upon them. Dependents, in their turn, should show the loyalty and affection appropriate either to junior members of the family or to faithful servants who have earned the right to become 'like members of the family'. The royal Christmas message has long been seen by those who hold this attitude as an uniquely appropriate expression of this national family sense at a time when family loyalty and affection are supposed to be celebrated. They would probably regard it as our most significant act expressive of national identity, far more so than the monarch's formal opening of Parliament.

Similarly, the characteristic appeal of the Conservative party throughout its history has been that it is the party of national unity. Many unsophisticated Conservatives, including some in very high places, still sincerely believe that members of other political parties are, by definition, dividers of the nation and guilty of family disloyalty. Without their own firm hold on the ancestral family loyalties to crown and church and property and the services, the British household would fall apart.

Nothing is easier in these days than to dismiss this idea with derision, a derision not unmixed with indignation when the blatantly ideological way in which it is used by some people of conservative temper is recalled. Let it be agreed that it provides a splendid justification for the continuing enjoyment of privilege by those who already possess it, whether in public service, industrial relations, social contacts, education or ecclesiastical affairs. It comes very hard on the family's poor relations, whether they be the Welsh or members of Commonwealth countries or even those English people themselves who are unlucky enough to have the wrong connections. Even among the accepted members of the household itself, great sacrifices are required of the weaker of them so that the dignity of the head, or of the oldest son, can be maintained, all, of course, for the sake of the family. Yet it is important to remember here that what is now being considered is an ideal, not its corruptions. One should not be blind to the way in which an ideal is corruptible, but if what has power to move people in the deep places where convictions are formed is ever to be understood, it is essential to begin by putting as generous an interpretation upon it as possible.

This is particularly the way of wisdom in this instance because most reflective people are so self-conscious and so censorious in relation to the long established traditions which they have inherited that they are in serious danger of underestimating the continuing power of this family ideal over large areas of British life. It is so pervasive that it can easily be evoked in conventional ways which are ready targets for disapproval or for mockery, yet in moments of crisis, its power stands sharply revealed. This is true even with many of those who would never openly confess its influence, as some people discovered to their surprise in the Second World War. Yet their reluctance to acknowledge this fact prevents many of those capable of doing so from stating and examining this ideal properly, thus continuing to leave its expression to the naive, the complacent and the self-centred.

It is hard for someone who is not in full sympathy with this ideal to do justice to it, but its strength and tenacity at its best are so great that it would be dishonest to discuss it as simply a confidence trick perpetrated by the traditional inheritors of power on their gullible retainers. Apart from anything else, it is held in different forms by people in many different sections of society and not only by those in positions of privilege. If the aristocracy are concerned to maintain their dynasty and their landed estates, the conservative middle classes are hardly less determined to maintain their kinship links and their family status. The admirable working-class desire both to hold fast to their traditional loyalties and style of life and, at the same time, to give their children a better chance springs from the same root. When the Queen speaks to such people on Christmas Day, they recognize that she is speaking for them as well as to them. This is as true on Deeside as it is on Thameside and, if it is not quite as universally true on Clydeside or Taffside, even there it produces a warm enough response.

There is no inherent reason why this ideal should be interpreted only in uncritically conventional terms. The artistic imagination has always been deeply attached to the past, and this is particularly true of the literary imagination. Dr F. R. Leavis claims to stand in the Puritan tradition in English life. The heirs of that tradition can be grateful to him for saying so at a time when such declarations are unfashionable and yet be left respectfully wondering whether he has placed himself aright. The world he so vividly evokes and contrasts with that of the present, the world of Thomas Tusser's *Five Hundred Points of Good Husbandry* and of the Wheelwright's Shop, the world even of his patron saint D. H. Lawrence, with its celebration of the allegedly 'organic' life of pre-industrial society, is the world of the conservative ideal rather than of Puritan radicalism. It is that of the closely-knit family with its strong relationships, rooted in the soil and responding with sympathy to the cycle of the natural year, with a loving attitude to its carefully-made possessions and a reluctance to throw anything away. The extraordinary beauty of the British landscape when it is unmarred by industrialization, and the deep attachment of many people, including those who have to spend much of their time in cities, to the way of life still partially carried on in the countryside, gives some indication of the continuing strength of this ideal. It probably remains true that no one can hope to do anything constructive which wins the consent of the majority of people in modern Britain who does not have a healthy respect for this family ideal. It may need to be extended and it may need to be qualified. It cannot be ignored and it cannot be deliberately affronted. Anybody who sets out to do no more than mock it may win a few quick laughs in these days, which may bring him profit and notoriety, but he is writing himself off as a serious political influence.

It is even more difficult to find a satisfactory name for the alternative British ideal than it is for the first. Puritan is a better word than Roundhead, but it does not quite fit because Puritanism has meant so many different things in the course of our history and because this ideal is shared by the Scots and the Welsh, while Puritanism was, in many respects, a distinctively English movement. The ideal of the radical Reformation, that which is prepared to consider 'the reformation of reformation itself' in Milton's phrase, might be the most precise, but the radical Reformation is a phrase used by church historians chiefly to refer to millenarian or revolutionary sects to the left of many who would acknowledge this ideal. Yet, again, however difficult it may be to name this attitude, its ideal is easily discernible. It is one of aspiration rather than of conservation. It has its eyes fixed much more on the coming kingdom of God than on the present kingdom of England and is much more readily prepared to alter the latter in the light of the former than to adjust its vision of the former to its experience of the latter. The vision of the coming kingdom is an abstract one, that of a kingdom not of this world, whose full realization must always lie in the future. Milton in his great prose pamphlets is as full of the pride of Englishness as his Cavalier opponents, if not more so, but it is the openness to the future, the readiness to change, the eagerness to discern and seize new opportunities, of the citizens of London which excite his imagination. Bunyan's pilgrim must always press on, forsaking those things which are behind, if he is to reach his goal. That goal is completely misunderstood if it is thought of as compensation in a vaguely specified hereafter for deprivation of experience here and now. To reach it in its fullness, Christian has to cross the river of death, but its light casts its radiance on his earthly pilgrimage and gives meaning and joy to his journey through life. The true Puritan objected to the use of visual images in worship not because they were beautiful but because, however beautiful they might be in themselves, they were a distraction from his vision of the coming King in his beauty, which far exceeds our best imagination in its life-enhancing power. This, he believed, was why earthly representations of the Deity were forbidden in Scripture.[7] True religion lay not in outward conformity, however decent, nor in the maintenance of a tradition, but in personal commitment which involved venture and risk. It was a matter of purity of heart, and that was to will one thing, in the phrase that Kierkegaard later used, to strive to be obedient to the living God at the core of one's being, even if it meant forsaking many of the things in this life which are most dear to one. It was this which gave British people the courage to leave their homeland and to establish overseas, notably in New England, colonies which were not reproductions of the traditional societies they had left but, as they believed, colonies of heaven.

Corruptio optimi pessima. When one has aspired to true purity of heart and inevitably failed to reach it, hypocrisy lies close at hand. And when the vision of one's high calling begins to fade and the tension of struggling to reach it to relax, it begins to be easier to content oneself with making the discipline which that struggle involves the end rather than the means of one's striving. That is the surest way, as the old Israel found, of making it a heavy burden rather than the easy yoke it was intended to be. There has been no shortage of people to point out how often this has happened to those who have stood in the Puritan tradition in British life, not least because that tradition itself produces articulate and critically-minded children who quickly let the world know when the burden presses heavily upon them. This makes it the more necessary to show the same sympathetic approach to this ideal as we have tried to show towards the other.

The dynamic nature of the Puritan ideal quickly creates problems for those who try to be faithful to it. They find it hard to stay still. When they try to do so, they become very bad conservatives, much more unattractive than their opposite numbers, whose education largely consists in making a virtue of conservatism and who are much more discriminating in what they conserve. But even as they move, it is difficult for them to maintain the vision of the kingdom of God with such clarity that they can be sure that they are continuing to move in the right direction. Their vision of a life beyond this life throws such fresh light on the possibilities of existence here and now that it promotes a great deal of secular activity. This activism of other-worldly Protestantism has often been commented upon, sometimes with the implication that it is self-contradictory. It is not self-contradictory, but it does confront those who engage in it with particularly strong temptations. Initially, this secular activity is in no way anti-religious. On the contrary, it is the attempt to express religious insight in the ordinary life of the world. This attempt, however, may easily become so absorbing, partly because of the very single-mindedness and power of concentration engendered by the search for purity of heart, that the heavenly vision becomes obscured and earthly visions, which claim the same authority, are substituted for it.

The way in which this has happened in economic life has received a great deal of attention from Max Weber onward, but the process can be seen much less ambiguously in British social and political life, on the liberal and 'progressive' sides. Much of this is the product of what Professor David Martin, echoing a phrase of T. E. Hulme, has called 'spilt religion',[8] and it has the strength and weakness of that religion very clearly marked upon it. It is idealistic and very distrustful of long-established power and the institutions which express it. It is unpretentious and impatient with all outward forms which do not clearly reflect an inner spirit. It is democratic in aspiration, although not always in achievement, because the majority often fail to meet its exacting standards. In all these ways, it expresses the strength of its Puritan origin. But it is also self-righteous, while being quick to condemn the same fault in others who do not share its beliefs. It divides the world too simply into the children of light and the children of darkness. It espouses the cause of the underdog but tends to despise him as soon as he achieves parity with others and then starts to behave like the rest of the pack. As it secularizes itself further, it becomes more and more conscious of its own superiority to the outlook of lesser mortals and more and more arbitrarily dogmatic about its own opinions. Perhaps it is only the liberalized heir of the radical reformation who can combine a prickly individualism which hates all established concentrations of power with a passionate belief in the collectivist ideals of socialism.

This is not said in order to make those who hold such views look merely ridiculous. These contradictions are often more apparent than real, and those who hold to both of them may not be fully consistent but are guided by a sure instinct. Liberty and equality are compatible ideals. This is the radical insight which conservatives fail to see, although they are compatible only in a context of fraternity, where people are able to cherish each other even while they differ. This is why they are bound to be held only in distorted form, and therefore to get in each other's way, when they are cut off from their religious source and inspiration. The chief weakness of British social and political life has long been that we have known both the Cavalier and the Roundhead ideals chiefly in their secularized and corrupted forms, with the irresistible force of the self-righteousness of the latter meeting the immoveable mass of the complacency of the former. We shall not conserve aright until we recapture what is authentic in our family ideal, and we shall not reform aright until we recapture a clear vision of a city which is to come. None of us will do either until we all learn a new sympathy with both ideals, because it is through the interaction of both at their best that the best of British life has always been found.

The attempt must now be made to specify what that best is. And the first quality to single out is the very one which makes such an attempt difficult and which makes most British people uneasy when it is made. It is that of reserve, the reserve which respects privacy. The deepest things in life are not to be exposed to the public view, where they might be freely handled or lightly talked about. The mystery of personal dignity must be safeguarded because personal responsibility is such a serious matter. Commitments which genuinely govern one's life are not easily formed, and the difficulty of articulating and explaining them properly may mean that one fails to do them justice and exposes them to insensitive criticism. Familiarity also breeds contempt, and no one should presume to enter into the most deeply personal areas of the life of another who is not prepared to pay the appropriate price in terms of his own personal involvement.

This respect for privacy has long been expressed in the manners and conversation of British civilization in a way which goes deeper than that of the formal etiquette of polite society. The purpose of many British conventions is both to facilitate relationships on less than the fully personal level, when those are the kinds of relationship the situation calls for, and to set barriers against casual or exploitative invasions of the fully personal dimension. All developed societies have such conventions, of course, but until very recently they have been cherished with particular care and sensitivity in British, and especially English, society, whether in relation to such relatively trivial matters as the observation of careful gradations in the way letters are begun or ended or more important ones such as those surrounding courtship and marriage. It may, perhaps, be unduly charitable to ourselves to wonder whether this reserve partly accounts for the reluctance of most British churchmen to embark on systematic theological study with the intensity or articulateness shown by, say, the Germans. If challenged, many of them may want to ask whether it is not presumptuous to analyse and argue about what we mean by God and would feel that it is more appropriate to show that godly fear which led the old Israel to hold her tongue when it came to uttering the divine name. It can be said with more confidence that, in a way which this loose-lipped age now finds hard even to understand, the reluctance of the best of the Victorians to speak at all about their sexual life was due not so much to prudery or a sense of guilt as to a clear-sighted recognition that certain matters are essentially private and to be dealt with only in a context of love and trust or of strictly confidential professional objectivity.

It is only in this kind of setting that the British ideal of the 'gentleman' can be best understood. Perhaps no word in British life has suffered a swifter and more complete decline than this. Up to the First World War it found widespread, if never universal, acceptance. Between the wars it became progressively less fashionable, and since the Second World War it has hardly been possible to mention it outside very limited circles without embarrassment. Since the sixties, it seems to have dropped out of the consciousness of most young people. The reason for this is only too obvious. Especially in its English form, it became the ideal only of a particular class, who came to assume that it was a status automatically possessed through birth and station, although it might just be possible to acquire it by a certain kind of education, and therefore that it carried with it privileges more than obligations.[9] Like so many other ideals, it became self-contradictory, constantly trying to justify itself in ungentlemanly ways, and finally, no doubt, it deserved to be laughed off the scene. Yet in the quiet places of many people's minds, the ideals of Chaucer's 'parfit gentil knyght', of Spenser's 'Faerie Queen' and of the kind of manhood represented by such figures as Sir Philip Sidney, remain authentic and powerful, even though a proper reserve makes them realize that it would be unwise to admit as much in public in these days.

The notion of the gentleman at its best was the Christian purification of the chivalric ideal. It recognized the facts of power and prestige, but insisted that they be used with deep respect for the human condition as such, for the fundamental equality of all people behind differences of rank or fortune or education. What people who themselves did not aspire to gentlemanly status called a 'real gentleman' was someone who took no advantage of a position of power. He was able even to accept a personal service in such a way that the personal dignity of the one who provided that service was not bruised but enhanced.

It is essential that this quality be rescued from its connections with class privilege because it is urgently necessary if modern urbanized life is not to become intolerable. The old distinction between 'gentle' and 'simple' people has fortunately disappeared, but the same kind of distinction is constantly reappearing in new forms, and it is a sure sign of a truly gentle spirit for those who are on the privileged side of the distinction to be quick to observe where it is arising and to avoid giving offence to those who believe their personal dignity to be threatened by it. The chief place where this distinction appears to be arising today is between those who have received higher education and the benefits it brings and those who have not. The amount of resentment the former cause among the latter because they contrive to make them feel inferior, often loudly proclaiming their attachment to ideals of equality while they do so, suggests that reflective people still have something to learn about how to behave from the old-fashioned ideals of gentlemanly conduct.

The fact that it is so clearly related to the use of power has meant that the gentlemanly ideal was developed most fully among the English, the most powerful nation in Britain. This does not mean that, if the ideal is to have any renewed vitality, it must only be in English terms. On the contrary, it provides a very good example of the way in which other elements in the British tradition can supplement and correct the English form of an ideal. English Free Church people and those from some industrial areas, and many Scots and Welsh, often having a good deal of power but being less associated with those social groups who have assumed that they are automatically gentlemanly, are in a better position to distinguish the reality from the form and see how it has to express itself in a rapidly changing world. The Scots can equal, and sometimes surpass, the English in showing dignified reserve, yet they can more easily do so without giving those they deal with a sense of social inferiority. The Welsh, who themselves can often do with a little English self-restraint, provide a warmth and spontaneity in the expression of fellow-feeling which do not come so readily to the more stiff-lipped English. This ability to adapt an ideal to changing circumstances is particularly important in a time when educational differences are so significant. The Welsh and the Scots have long realized that education is now a major road to power and influence, and are more aware than the English of the dangers of social divisiveness that it brings.[10] Both countries have become accustomed to having many graduates from poor families, and people in them are aware of the adjustments which are needed to avoid new forms of social *apartheid* and to reaffirm communal solidarity. This is why they can do service to British society as a whole if they can refurbish what is distinctive in their ideals of what respect for quality in a context of equality really means. If nationalist movements in both countries could see this as part of their task, it would help everybody. We need a Scots or a Welsh style of safeguarding the mystery of human dignity in situations where education leads to social advantage, styles that supplement those associated with Oxbridge which have for so long been the British norm. The novels of Emyr Humphreys indicate what this might mean in Welsh terms and, despite all the myths busily propagated in the television age about the alleged 'establishment-mindedness' of the BBC in the Reith era, it was the Glaswegian respect for the personal dignity of ordinary people, which carried the conviction that they had both the right to expect and the ability to enjoy the best of which the best were capable, which helped to make the BBC the genuinely educational and socially unifying influence it was in that time.

The second quality which reflects the British ideal is closely related to respect for privacy but the focus is different. It is that of modesty. The British gift for understatement is a frequent source of amused and wondering foreign comment, especially by Americans whose national gifts lie in other directions. It can, of course, be no more than an affectation of speech but, when it is genuine, it is a sure sign of maturity and self-confidence. When Emerson wrote his *Traits of the English*, based on his observation in the early days of Victorian expansion, modesty was emphatically not a quality which he was able to detect in our midst. We have had to learn through hard experience, as America herself appears to have to now, that it is always unwise to think more highly of oneself than one ought to think and that sobriety, and with it the refusal to over-reach oneself in success, is the way of realism and of wisdom. If we ourselves, or our fathers before us, have achieved anything in the world, it was due as much to good fortune or the mercy of providence or the efforts of others as it was to anything we or they have done. The margin between success and failure is often quite small, and the distinction between even our best achievements and those of our neighbours in the sight of God is so slight that for us to make much of them is to invite ridicule.

This is why in British public life there is such a healthy distrust of 'the cult of personality'. It may be acceptable for people in the world of professional entertainment to be built up in this way and to exact their due measure of uncritical adulation, but this itself indicates that they are not serious people to be trusted with serious business. A professional man quickly loses the esteem of his fellows if he indulges in self-advertisement, and more ambiguous characters like politicians and clerics, who cannot escape being in the public eye, still have to walk carefully lest they become 'over-exposed'. The English in particular, and here they do differ from many Scots and Welsh, react sharply against anyone who indulges in more eloquence than the occasion demands. The highly dramatic preacher and the pontificating judge and the soldier who makes fighting speeches are treating their auditors as admirers rather than mature colleagues and they are rarely forgiven, especially if they go on for too long. They prompt questions like, 'Who do they think they are and what are they trying to prove? Let them say what is expected of them and shut up.' Such people are believed to imply that their persons are more important than their office. The distinction between genuine testimony based on conviction, which may justify a personal reference, and mere salesmanship is a fine one, but it is one which the British intelligence at its best has long been accustomed to draw. Those who cherish the British ideal would argue that it is essential to draw it with increasing firmness in an age when the salesman becomes ever more brazenly vociferous.

Here again, the distinctive qualities of the people of the separate parts of Britain at their best are needed if the most it is to be made of the ideal of modesty. In English life, the Puritan tradition has emphasized directness, unpretentiousness and 'the plain style'. Its word is its bond, its yea yea and its nay nay. It dislikes dressing up and has a horror of graven images. This means that it hates the modern cult of the manufacture of 'images' and the subtle forms of self-advertisement which call themselves 'public relations'. This attitude is very close to the sober concern for intrinsic quality and the emphasis on the self-effacement of the individual which is characteristic of the conservative Anglican tradition.[11] The Scottish emphasis on competence, reliability and strict accountability, and dislike of extravagance, also fits in well with these. And while their best friends could hardly claim that a dislike of exaggeration is a Welsh characteristic, it is worth remembering that that gift for exaggeration is normally reserved for fields in which the exercise of a free imagination is appropriate. Nowhere in these islands is there a greater distrust for the values of glossy commercialism than in the most Welsh parts of Wales, nor a more ready appreciation of unpretentious personal modesty.

As always happens when people are at their best, it is remarkable how similar to each other those representing the differing strains in British life are when they are arguing self-critically about what they should do for the common good. The recently published transcripts of the internal discussions of the Little Gidding community in the seventeenth century are very similar in tone and general attitude,[12] despite the marked difference in context, to the famous Putney Debates of the New Model Army in 1647. This is why it is important to do what we have become so reluctant to do in modern Britain, to discuss openly our deepest beliefs with each other, even when initially we may seem to be far apart. The more deeply we dig, the closer we get to each other.

Thirdly, the British ideal is one of fair play. The sporting metaphor has long been overworked beyond the point of utter banality, with the result that, like the ideal of the gentleman, it evokes derision more readily than assent today, but this should not be allowed to conceal the depth of the conviction which it tries to express. For what people mean when they speak of 'fair play' is an insight which combines realism about the human condition, a sense of justice and an awareness of our dependence on each other. It recognizes that there are differences between people, and that a great deal of the interest in life lies in measuring those differences. It also accepts the fact that the achievement of excellence often carries with it a necessary element of competitive struggle. This is the way mankind has evolved, and even the most exalted experiences of love and unity cannot therefore transform instincts on all levels overnight, as utopian idealists imagine. Yet because we have moved away from the law of the jungle, we are able increasingly to organize our competitive struggles with each other more and more in the form of play, and less and less in that of war to the death. This need not take the heat of effort and the joy of victory and the misery of defeat out of those struggles, but it does set them within firm and tolerable limits. It takes away the frenzy and the destructiveness and the threat of chaos come again. We compete, but not in such a way that no holds are barred. For the sake of the continuance of the game itself, and also as a reminder that competition between the children of God is never more than a game, we abide by the rules. And the rules themselves must be fair. There must be equality before them, for the strong as for the weak, but no less for the weak as for the strong. Fairness may demand a system of handicapping to ensure that all start on equal terms, but to bend the rules, once established, for the sake of the weak, is to treat the weak as less than mature and to take away the savour of any victory they might win. At the end of a good game, victor and vanquished should be united in enjoyment of the contest and appreciation of each other.

To claim that this ideal is peculiarly British would be insufferably smug, but most of the world's most popular team games were devised in Britain, and it has been more widely influential here than in most countries. It certainly stands in marked contrast to ideas which have had currency in continental Europe but which have taken little root here. Like Nietzsche, those who hold this ideal recognize 'the will to power' but, unlike Nietzsche, they recognize both the dangers and limitations of that will and, especially the possibilities of a more creative response on the part of those who do not obtain the chief prizes. The notion of 'a good loser' is as remote from Nietzsche's view of the world as anything could be but it is essential to the ideal of fair play. The good loser knows that he operates within a context of equality and that with a little luck he might possibly win, so that he is free from Nietzsche's 'resentment', and therefore from the need to develop a 'slave-morality' with its attendant priestcraft. Having given of his best, he has not lost his self-respect nor the respect of his opponent, so he 'lives to fight another day' with his spirit unimpaired. This is why, to most readers, Nietzsche's account of Christianity (which actually seems much nearer to modern liberalism than to the faith of the New Testament) seems as one-sided as his account of aristocracy, whatever marginally valid insights it might contain. Believing that God was dead and that a man with divine pretensions had to take his place, he took human destiny too seriously to see human creativity in terms of the metaphor of a game. Whatever their theological limitations, the British do at least know that man is not God and that there is something ridiculously pretentious about human attempts to ape the divine creativity. The creative activity of those who are themselves creatures is more analogous to the play of children with materials and in a setting provided by their elders than that primal activity of bringing something out of nothing which believers ascribe to God.[13]

This ideal of fair play is, in its turn, linked to another more elusive one which British people hold in high esteem, that of moderation. It is very close to the quality of *epieikes* to which Paul refers in Philippians 4.5, which is variously translated 'moderation', 'forbearance', 'toleration', 'courtesy' or, best of all, 'magnanimity'. This is the quality which most clearly expresses that balance in tension which Ian Nairn found exemplified in St Paul's Cathedral. It is, above all, a positive quality, a quality of strength and not of weakness. Those who possess it avoid absolutes, whether in religion, politics or culture, not out of lack of conviction but because they have learnt through hard experience that it is precisely when we are most deeply convinced of our own rightness that we are most likely to go astray. Their equally convinced opponent is likely to see some part of the truth, and he has a right to express it and follow it as best he can. If their interests clash in doing so, conflict may be inevitable, but it should be limited and the possibility of reconciliation kept open. Men are not gods, and the corollary of this is that when they disagree, their opponents are not devils. True moderation recognizes that all quarrels are family quarrels and must be kept in due proportion because we are committed to each other and must go on living together.

This quality finds expression along the whole range of British life. It does so most clearly in the way the political party system has evolved at the national level and, in particular, in the conventions and procedures of the House of Commons itself. The office of the Speaker of the House, who is much more than a chairman, exemplifies it most clearly of all. But it has also become part of the characteristically British style of life and is a good deal of what we mean when we speak vaguely of 'freedom' or even 'democracy' and contrast it with what prevails in totalitarian states. It finds expression most clearly in the way we treat those who differ from us. Anyone who tries to ride roughshod over others without regard to their situation or susceptibilities probably evokes less admiration in Britain than in almost any other large-scale society, and the more he flaunts his success, the more unpopular he becomes. Power and privilege should not merely be made more acceptable by being politely exercised. The utmost restraint should be shown in their use, and if they are not involved at all, so much the better. Thus, the Queen and the Royal Family are widely admired in Britain. The number of real dissentients, even in these irreverent days, is small. Yet, as they appear to understand very well, the price of their popularity is that they constantly reassure the rest of the community that 'they are just like you and me', while yet retaining their proper royal dignity. The English 'love a lord'—the Scots and the Welsh are markedly less affectionate—but only if he does not act like one. The most admired of the armed services is the Navy, but this is partly because it is the 'silent service' and goes about its business with the minimum of fuss and pomp. 'Our policemen are wonderful,' but only to the extent that they are able to conceal their authority. If, as Norman Mailer says, 'a good cop is a work of art', we can be justly proud of our collection, but this is largely because of their skill in judging how little force is needed to achieve a desired end, as advocates of totalitarian causes who try to provoke them into acts of public violence understand very well.

Despite all that has been said, English readers will probably still feel that each of these ideals is more distinctively English than generally British. It is, of course, true that because the English are in the large majority in Britain and because it is in London, the national capital, that the public scene is busiest and receives most attention, institutions located in England provide the best illustrations of them. Yet Scotland and Wales, and the 'non-Establishment' English, contribute much that is distinctive to the way in which these ideals are held, without which there could be little of the essential balance in tension within them.

For example, English reserve and modesty might be so inhibited and withdrawn that they would be in danger of fading into mere complacency without that strong sense of purpose which is more characteristic of the Lowland Scots. There are honourable Scots elements in the ancestry of Evelyn Waugh, but they seem to have been effectively buried in the creation of his ideal Englishman, Guy Crouchback. One could imagine him existing in the kind of Sussex village, well away from the main lines, in which Hilaire Belloc came to rest, but it is hard to think of him in any Scottish milieu south of the Highland line. It remains more true of the Scots than of most of the Southern English that they know that they are 'strangers and pilgrims' on the earth and that, therefore, the individual has to take the risk of showing the invidious independence of spirit involved in trying to do some new thing.

Similarly, Scots high seriousness qualifies the kind of sense of moderation which the English possess. Their interests in matters of 'ultimate concern' in these days can be exaggerated. When Paul Tillich, the author of that phrase, gave the Gifford lectures at the University of Aberdeen, the audiences were as small as they would have been at an English provincial university. Yet the Scots remain more likely than most of the English to see that there are certain issues which cannot be resolved simply by a little give and take here and there and a sensible readjustment of perspective, while the continuities are preserved. They put a little iron, a little intellectual rigour, into British moderation which in its English, and especially in its Anglican form, it needs. The 'moderator' who earns the respect of a Scottish Kirk assembly is the one who not only sees that things are done decently and in order but also sees that they are done.

There are also two wider considerations which affect not so much the nature of the ideals themselves as the context in which they are held, and therefore the degree of effectiveness with which they can be implemented. One is the fact already noted, that the characteristic Scottish spirit is more democratic than the English. All communities have their forms of snobbery and Scotland is not free of them. Even the very democratic Welsh have a cult of university degrees. But the notion that 'a man's a man for a' that' is not entirely a matter of bibulous Burns-night rhetoric. The British ideal in its dominant English form has only managed to express itself effectively in upper- and middle-class life, and those who have tried sincerely to live by it have not shown much skill in conveying it to working-class people in a way which enables them in their turn to exercise an independent judgment on the way they try to realize it. This has to be qualified only in those areas of England, like parts of the North, which are most like Scotland. Working-class people often have better living conditions in the prosperous South than they do in Scotland, but they are likely to have much more definite minds of their own in Scotland.

The other is that the Scots, having to live very consciously in two nations simultaneously, have precisely that perspective on British life which the English find so hard to acquire. They have equally strong inherited loyalties, sometimes more passionately held than English ones, but they have to be defined in relation to other loyalties, and the act of definition limits them. They cannot escape the recognition that they live in a wider world, and that the whole world does not revolve around these islands. This helps to give them the ability to commend the British ideal to people of other nations which those people are able to accept without being compelled to feel that they have also to accept English institutions and conventions. This makes it the more essential that, in the kind of world into which we have moved today, Scots people should see their international responsibilities in British and not simply in narrowly Scottish terms.

The Welsh contribution to the British ideal may be less pronounced than the Scots because Wales is smaller, poorer and more overwhelmed by her proximity to her larger neighbour, but her very smallness and poverty may themselves make it essential. Although, among the nations of the world, the English are not particularly numerous, they do not think of themselves as a little people and have difficulty in understanding how things look to little people. Few Welshmen would feel at home in Nairn's St Paul's, and this reveals limitations in their outlook which they could learn how to overcome from the English, but not many English people, and very few of the 'establishment' English, would feel at home in the intimate, informal atmosphere of a Welsh chapel.[14] It is a Welsh virtue to be able vividly to enter into the pity of the human condition without self-pity, so that they can be genuinely sympathetic. The Welsh word for 'small', *bach*, is also the diminutive of affection. A familiar Welsh description of someone deserving sympathy is the expressive phrase, 'a poor little dab'. No 'poor little dab' would be left out in the cold for very long in any Welsh valley. If the Welsh could do with a little more of the English upper-class 'stiff upper lip', the latter's reserve needs no less to be tempered with that warm and ready identification with human need which the Welsh can offer. These islands, which are always on the point of emerging from the temperate into the frigid zone, depend on this soft Western breeze to take the edge off the Viking rigour of the East.

Similarly, the Welsh lyrical gift helps to give colour and imaginative power to the British ideal. The seriousness combined with tenderness and the distrust of the abstracting power of the intellect which D. H. Lawrence advocated finds its most natural expression in Welsh poetry and culture, without the traces of malice and cruelty which disfigured them in Lawrence. The

Welsh live close to the earth, but their sweetest songs are those which sing of heaven, and this purifies, while it does not constrict, their attitude to earthly affection.

Wales has the defects of these qualities in abundance. Her lyrical gift runs easily into sentimentality, her sense of littleness can become an introverted tribalism and her warmth can lose itself in undisciplined sensuality. There is a strain of weakness in the Welsh character, as in the Irish and in that of the Highlands, although it is probably due more to long-standing poverty and depression than to anything distinctively Celtic. This helps to justify the moral austerity of those leaders who, since the Methodist revival, have striven to raise the sights of the Welsh people, and it underlines how much they need the sympathetic support of other peoples of Britain.

This is true all along the line. The English, the Scots and the Welsh need the best of each other to bring out the best in themselves. This in no way minimizes the right of each to assert their own identities. On the contrary, it requires that that right should be fully exercised. But it says a great deal about the manner of its exercise, and its context. To return to the example of John Reith, his high seriousness and dedicated sense of purpose would have been disproportionate, and perhaps ineffective, operating in a purely Scottish setting. An independent Scottish Broadcasting Corporation run by the young John Reith is an awe-inspiring thought, but not one capable of inspiring any other emotion than that of awe. But coming into the more open and flexible society of London, where the dangers of 'metropolitan wastage' are so much greater but where there was much more room for a big man with convictions to move about and get things done without over-whelming everyone else, he was worth his considerable weight in gold. Yet the point to be emphasized was that it was Scottish qualities in an English context which did this. For John Reith to have become simply a copy of an English-type pillar of the London Establishment could have turned him into no more than a Cosmo Gordon Lang. Scottish and Welsh Nationalists believe that all their compatriots who participate in wider British life are bound to suffer that fate. The evidence proves the contrary, and it is essential to the continuing health of all parts of these islands that it should continue to do so.

3   *The limitations of the British ideal*

What has been described is the ideal for conduct in their own society which the majority of reflective people in Britain hold. It is an admirable ideal, realized imperfectly as all ideals are, but one which has required a great deal of self-discipline, sacrifice and painfully acquired wisdom to reach the measure of realization which it has achieved. Yet is it enough? It would be worrying if we thought it was. Those who have studied the New Testament should understand that it is when people are at their best and can make a fair show of conforming to the ideals by which they claim to live that they are at their most vulnerable. No society can escape problems, and the more lively and successful a society is, the more subtle and difficult its problems become. When people are happy together and have achieved a social consensus, and when even minorities enjoy a reasonable measure of toleration, it is hard to avoid complacency. Things then begin to go wrong. Those who benefit most from the society's prosperity become insensitive in their complacency to the new needs which are always arising and refuse to make the adjustments which have to be made if the consensus is to be maintained and justice is to continue to be done. They feel threatened and become defensive. Meanwhile the critical young (and it appears to be a law of life in self-conscious modern society that the more successful a community is the more it engenders a critical spirit in its young people) become disgruntled and, lacking power and not realizing how hard-won are the benefits they take for granted, turn away from the ideals of their fathers. This is why it is important both to scrutinize those ideals in the light of changing experience and also to recognize that they themselves are likely to be inadequate.

It is not easy to detect where one's own ideals are inadequate, either for the young or for the old, especially when failure to live up to those we already acknowledge is so obvious as it is today. All our energies, most people would feel, are needed for trying to live up to the ideals we already have without worrying about others which we might possess. That family feeling which so many British people cherish is expressed imperfectly enough in our dealings with each other but hardly at all in our relations with nations less fortunate than ourselves. Despite all the eloquence which has been expended on the subject for generations, the rich still get richer and the poor poorer. This is true even in our own country, where some efforts are made to redress the balance, but it is glaringly so as between the 'developed nations', of which we are still one, and the 'third world'. We do not give anything like enough help to poorer countries and admit immigrants from them only grudgingly and when they are economically necessary to us, while we condone, even if we do not actively support, unjust régimes in Africa and other parts of the world, for which we have a direct responsibility. We plunder the earth for irreplaceable natural resources, while we pollute the atmosphere, land and water in the selfish pursuit of an ever-increasing gross national product, criticizing ourselves only when we fail to increase it fast enough to satisfy our own voracious appetites and to keep up with our competitors. In all this, we yet like to see ourselves as worthy custodians of the British heritage.

Some parts of this familiar indictment may be overdrawn, but it has enough truth in it to give urgency to demands for radical reform. No one can deny, for example, that the momentum has gone out of the effort to achieve greater social and economic equality which arose out of the Second World War.[15] The sense of civic obligation on the part of the main interest groups in the community has also sharply declined. Management blames the unions and the unions management, and those in education blame businessmen and businessmen denounce students, but very few people, and no organized group, are prepared to make any sacrifice for the public good. There is little consolation to the Christian preacher who is devoted to Britain to see how much recent history has confirmed the ancient truth that selfishness breeds selfishness and that, unless someone is prepared to pay the price of breaking out of the nexus of selfishness, everyone is dragged down by it.

Yet, while these matters must remain our most immediate

preoccupation, we shall probably not succeed even in being faithful to our acknowledged ideals unless we see some fresh things about our present situation which enable us to see those ideals themselves in a different light and to find new resources for trying to realize them. Are there any neglected places where they might be found?

One may be found in relation to the kind of self-criticism which is necessary even when we try to serve others. Most people would argue that healthy personal and social fulfilment is to be found through such service. But is the matter as simple as that? How can those who have inherited the privileges and attitudes of power learn genuinely to serve and not covertly to dominate? We have seen that the gentlemanly ideal helps those who enjoy privilege and exercise power to do so in ways which do not violate the personal integrity of others, but this question carries the matter further because it implies that it may sometimes be necessary to set aside privilege in order to make oneself available to meet the needs of others. The temptation is to assume that the purity of one's own motivation gives an automatic assurance that one's action is for the best. This leads people to blunder into situations without sufficient regard for the outlook and circumstances of those whom they are trying to help. As the USA discovered so disastrously in Vietnam, this can make a situation worse and not better. No position is more invidious than that of the rich man who comes bearing gifts, unless it is that of the rich man's children, who have seen the dangers of their parent's action and therefore try to avoid the inescapable responsibilities of privilege and power, as again many young Americans have tried to do.

Is there any way out of this dilemma for modern Britain? If the first temptation was the stronger in the days of imperial expansion, the second is stronger today, when we are self-critical without having the confidence or courage to act. What would be the best way out is clear enough. It is to be compelled to do an unavoidable job so large and so demanding that most people are prepared to forget their own short-term interests in getting on with it. This happened to Britain between 1940 and the early 1950s and it produced the social revival which issued in the 'welfare state'

legislation and the outburst of educational expansion which
followed, but which quickly petered out in the febrile self-
consciousness and triviality of the sixties. If we were able to
dedicate ourselves to the service of the under-developed world a
similar release of energy might be achieved, without the brutality
and destructiveness of war, but the necessary amount of dedication
and seriousness of purpose simply do not seem to be available in
modern British life. The inward assurance, the generosity of
temper and the overflowing energy which such action would
require, of the kind possessed by the best of the Christian missionaries of the last hundred years, have departed. There is no reason
to suppose that belonging to the EEC, which means joining forces
with nations in a similar situation to our own but with much
weaker traditions of international service, is likely to tap sources of
new power which might enable us to forget ourselves in the
service of a great cause.

If this is the case, the only place where the British can look is
inside their own life to see what they can learn from the failures as
well as the successes of their history. This, in any case, is the right
place to begin. Nothing can be offered to other nations which they
will be eager to receive unless what we already possess wins their
admiration and respect. As professional Christian workers know,
it is peculiarly enervating to move among others as one who wishes
to serve when they show a marked disinclination to accept one's
services. This is why others are more effectively served by example
than by direct action, especially in matters which concern their
own dignity and sense of responsibility. In the past, and this
includes the quite recent past, the admiration and emulation of the
rest of the world have been won and inspired by British reserve
and modesty and fair play and magnanimity. If we can regain these
qualities and also show how to achieve equality without the sacrifice
of excellence, as we began to be able to do for a time after the
Second World War, or if we can begin to look to the future in the
conviction that we can make this country a better place than it has
been in the past, the world will again begin to beat a path to our
door to learn from us. It is no longer as easy as it was to export our
internal frustrations. That is the dubious privilege reserved for the

top nation, and America has been busily doing it for some time. They have to be resolved in our own life, and it is only as this is done that new possibilities will begin to emerge.

Is it too late? Many voices, both within and outside Britain, say that it is. That there are signs of decadence in modern Britain is undeniable. It does sometimes look as though mobility, triviality and metropolitan wastage are at last undermining the strength and stability of British life to an extent which was not even achieved by the Industrial Revolution and two world wars. Yet to talk of irrevocable decline is too sweeping and certainly premature. Britain, like other advanced countries, has looked decadent over large areas of her life in the past and has recovered. There was little to enthuse over in her life in the late twenties and early thirties, and yet she managed the revival of the forties and early fifties. The oft-noted pluralism of the modern world means that trends which point in different directions exist simultaneously alongside each other. Even the sixties saw a fresh outburst of intelligent concern over pollution and the 'quality of life' which may hold great promise for the future.

Decline is not automatic but, by the same token, neither is revival. The British people need to have at least these two new and different attitudes before it can become a possibility.

First, much harder and more honest thought about British society and its institutions is necessary, thought of the kind which issues in action. The most unrealistic of all the aspirations expressed in singing Blake's 'Jerusalem' on British occasions is that which affirms, 'I will not cease from mental fight.' Most of us never started. Much of the trouble about where we should go and what we should do is caused by intellectual confusion produced by lack of intellectual effort. Of course, the effort required is more than intellectual if imaginations are to be properly kindled and action taken, but British people have become so weak in thinking about their society, and so complacent about their weakness, that it is this which needs initially to be most stressed. Even those ideals we acknowledge are held in a slack and easy-going way and therefore without that tension which we have seen to be essential if the balance of British life is to be creative.

This means carrying the debate about 'the state of the nation' on to a much deeper level than has ever been achieved except briefly during the nineteenth century under the leadership of Gladstone and Disraeli and in the 1940s. The British system of two-party government, with the possibilities of informed parliamentary criticism and of the ready availability of an alternative government which it provides, is an essential safeguard of our liberties, but it has long been obvious that our politics need better statements of the radical and conservative options than the present parties are able to offer if public life is to continue to be healthy. These cannot be provided by hard-pressed politicians alone. We have many excellent limited studies of particular aspects of British life, but it is the larger issues from which we avert our eyes. More people need to probe more deeply into the roots of communal vitality, to examine how commitments are born and how they are nurtured and expressed. Above all, we need to see how, on the one hand, the virtue of loyalty can be cultivated and, on the other, those of self-criticism and tolerance of others who have different loyalties.

This is the responsibility of all reflective people who accept public positions and support, all Coleridge's 'clerisy', and they must carry it further than most of them seem prepared to do. For example, in an effort to do this in his book *The Offshore Islanders*,[16] Mr Paul Johnson makes a moving re-affirmation of the liberal ideal with which it is hard to disagree. He expresses it in terms very close to those in which we have spoken of some aspects of the British ideal, although he follows more closely than we might its statement by Mill and the philosophical radicals. He points out that the liberal ideal was one which aims at 'improvement' rather than 'progress' or even 'reform'. He says that what has happened in the twentieth century is not that this ideal has been tried and found wanting, but that it has been 'starved of enthusiasm, conviction, intellectual nourishment and followers'. This may be true, but what he does not ask is why it has been starved in this way. The answer to that question may tell us a great deal about where we have gone wrong. A Christian would say that the reason is that this admirable ideal is not self-generating. There has been an

opportunity in this generation to try to engender all that Mr
Johnson wants without reference to other criteria than those of
liberal ideals themselves through the great expansion of education,
and particularly higher education. But as Mr Johnson himself goes
on to say, it is in the universities themselves that we have seen the
most violent, intolerant and ignorant attacks on the liberal ideal.

When intellectuals reject liberalism they do not take refuge in scepticism (which is itself an element in the liberal method). They do not
believe in nothing. On the contrary they believe in anything.[17]

What he does not ask is how they came to lose their faith and
how they can regain it. Those familiar with the language of the New
Testament would see post-liberal man as like a house swept and
garnished into which seven legions of devils, whose predecessors
have been kept out by strongly held convictions in the past, have
come rushing.

In this situation, those who hold to the liberal ideal have to look
to its origins. Whatever their own present attitude to those origins,
where they are to be found is undeniable. It is the religious faith
of the Reformation in its various forms, which was based on a
fresh understanding of God's dealings with men, one which gave
them courage to break with old formulations and patterns and
made them willing to venture into unknown territory. This produced intense conviction and, as with all intense convictions which
had to assert itself against opposition, it found it hard to be tolerant,
although someone like Cromwell very nearly managed it even in a
time of intense strain and provocation. As it secularized itself by
moving out into the world of everyday affairs, however, it
inevitably became less radical and less intolerant and issued in a
very sober and practical idealism, which expressed itself precisely
in that 'improving' attitude so much admired by Johnson. As we
have seen, the Scots provide the most striking examples of this,
but those Englishmen of similar conviction shared their attitude.
The Protestant faith which lay at its root is weaker today than in
the past, but it is still present and, as we have seen, its influence
can be clearly traced in the background and personal histories of
many of those who exemplify this attitude in our public life.

If the liberal ideal is to be replenished, these two points about it must be seen. The first is that it is based on a vision not of the past but of the future. It is not in the strict sense a 'millenarian' vision, for these tend to over-simplify, in the way Marxist restatements of hope for the future do, the relation between this world and a world to come. They try to define too directly in terms of this life a state of affairs which is only possible beyond this life even at its best. Nor is it 'utopian', which is a speculative vision of an ideal state which does not face with the necessary urgency the question of how one gets from here to there. It is eschatological in the New Testament sense. It is a vision of the End, which must be the goal of our striving, one defined in terms of the understanding of this life, its possibilities and its limitations, made clear in the life and teaching of Jesus Christ. It cannot be fully realized while the basic conditions of life on this earth remain as they are, but it conditions and controls the way we live on this earth, determining the way in which we are moving while at the same time making us see that our best efforts to be faithful to the vision will be fragmentary and temporary. Because it is of the essence of this vision that it comes from beyond any present possiblities, it comes in its own time and way and cannot be induced by any effort on our part, however fervently we may long for it. If it is not present, however, something can be done about its absence. The alternative is neither scepticism nor that feverish search for any kind of commitment of which Mr Johnson complains.

This is where the second point becomes relevant. The liberal ideal can only be effectively held by those who have the conservative attitude. No authentic vision of the future can come except on the basis of a positive appreciation of the past, and often as a reinterpretation of it.[18] This is why it is essential to hold both sides in tension. The best radical is the natural conservative who is driven to become a radical by charity, the same charity which leads him to cherish and enjoy the best fruits of the past. Without this, the vision of the future quickly becomes distorted into a millenarianism which leads to violence and intolerance, to the revolution which uproots without rebuilding unless, as in modern Russia, elements from the past are surreptitiously reintroduced into society. Alternatively, it trivializes itself into mere utopianism, which dreams of an ideal state and makes a few rhetorical gestures in its direction while it enjoys a feeling of moral superiority and seeks compensation by fiercely criticizing all society's improvers as appeasers. Those who have a vision of the future which they hope to realize must be identified with their own society, must love it, understand its institutions, steep themselves in the wisdom of its past, appreciate how precious any inherited achievement of civilization is and how ambiguous, and costly, any venture into the unknown has to be. Under the constraint of their vision they may set out to be revolutionaries, but they will quickly discover the element of self-delusion in such ambitions and know that the most they can hope to be is 'improvers'. This will have the salutary effect of making them hate violence and intolerance without impairing their ability to take decisive action. Their liberalism will not be that 'soft' liberalism so despised by the self-righteously committed, but a qualification of their own strong convictions by the recognition that wisdom was neither born nor is likely to die with them. This will help them to see not only that others have rights but also that their convictions deserve to be expressed and heeded, even when they conflict sharply with their own. This alone makes it possible to keep society open in the way the liberal ideal itself demands.

Yet the dependence of the liberal ideal on the conservative attitude in no way implies, as conservatives like to suppose, that therefore conservatism is enough. The dangers of conservatism left to itself are even worse, because the facts of life do act as a check on the visionary radical. If he wishes to do anything, he has to take account of them. The conservative, however, is generally in a position of privilege. He finds things good and wants to keep them that way. It is only when he is goaded by the radical that he is stirred out of his natural complacency and lethargy. When he is, his first reaction is simply to defend what he has and to interpret any proposed change in a negative and insensitive way. This is why no one can trust himself to be a conservative unless he struggles to maintain conversation with the radical on as profound a level as possible. It is the responsibility of education (and all good education has, by definition, to be conservative) to be 'liberal' in this sense, to see why the past cannot properly be appropriated except in the context of being open to fresh possibilities. Yet the radical in his turn must define his vision in a way which kindles the imagination, so that the conservative is stirred not into mere reaction but into a fresh and more profound restatement of the traditional wisdom, to the benefit of the radical's attempt to realize his vision in practice.

This process has conspicuously failed to take place in modern British politics, and is the cause of many of its current ills. It would be unfair to attach much blame to practising politicians for this. Those who, in academies and studies and pulpits, should be looking at politics in a larger perspective, cannot escape blame so lightly. British politics since the war have been dominated by the promotion of economic 'growth' as a self-evidently good thing. Labour's vision of the 'godly commonwealth' has increasingly come to be thought of only in crassly economic terms and the Conservative party, on the other hand, seems to have surrendered its responsibility for preserving the best fruits of our heritage and maintaining the continuity of British institutions in its desire to become the servant of the revolutionary force of industrialization and the caprices of the world of finance. Entry into Europe might possibly have sparked off a profounder debate, but even that has been turned into a wrangle about whether or not it will be to our economic advantage. The Scots and the Welsh, as we have seen, could bring fresh insight into the British debate, but the Welsh appear increasingly to content themselves with the narrow and over-simplified issue of using political power to promote the Welsh language, and the tempting prospect of North Sea oil has encouraged many Scots to new heights of economic chauvinism. The belated expression of widespread concern for the environment and 'the quality of life' may be the augury of better things, but much more profound thought is needed before our politics can improve.

A better debate is necessary, as are the higher standards for communal life which might issue from that debate. Anyone who reads modern British history has a strong sense of unrealized possibilities which have hovered on the edges of the nation's life, of things which made a difference but never enough of a difference to achieve a decisive breakthrough. This was particularly true in Elizabethan times, before the division between Cavaliers and Roundheads. To begin with, a great deal was achieved, but then the break came and the tension between the two sides was never again as fruitful as it might have been. The Massachusetts Bay colonists had to leave old England to build a New England as an example of what a truly reformed godly commonwealth should be. Their achievement has had enormous consequences for mankind, but the fact that they had to leave meant that they lacked vital elements in the British tradition which old England preserved, with the result in our time that self-conscious direct descendants of those early colonists like T. S. Eliot and Robert Lowell have had to go backwards in order to try to recover those elements. When, in the nineteenth century, the two strains came into significant contact again, notably in the great figure of Gladstone, the most profoundly thoughtful of modern British political leaders, they had been separated for too long, and too many new and incalculable forces were abroad in the world, for the result to have been as creative as the situation demanded.

A similar sense of unrealized possibilities begins by now to develop as one looks back on the period from 1940 to about 1960. We were a more united nation than we had been since late Elizabethan times, but although strenuous efforts were made, which have not yet been fully appreciated or recorded,[19] to make us think more deeply about our heritage and our future, they proved insufficient, and most thinking about the rebuilding of British life concentrated only on such matters as rehousing, the extension of social service benefits and the extension of educational opportunity. This is not a moment when anyone can hope to do better in the way of positive redefinition than their predecessors were able to in a time more conducive to sober reflection, but there are one or two places where the way in which standards have fallen have become only too obvious.

First, they have fallen in relation to communication. This refers to more than to what is today called the 'communications industry' or the 'media', of the press and broadcasting. It is human intercourse on the level of the the public expression of ideas. Here new standards of integrity are needed for new situations. Under modern conditions, evil communication does more than corrupt good manners. It weakens the very fabric of society, which is more than ever dependent on effective communication. Romantic individualism has made much of the integrity of the artist, and this has been transfoimed into the professional communicator's claim to a right of unlimited freedom of expression, with the assumption that his own integrity is unchallengeable. But it is obvious, and needs very strongly to be reasserted, that he can only claim that right when he shows respect for the integrity of the people whom he addresses at least equal to that which he demands for his own. His approach must be the reverse of that advocated by many advertisers. He must not talk down or appeal, whether overtly or covertly, to avarice, vanity or prejudice. He must not mislead or seduce, or if, as an artist, he may sometimes appear to do so, it must only be in order to uncover by indirect means an aspect of the truth which might otherwise go undetected. He should combine the Puritan's insistence on making his 'yea yea' and his 'nay nay' with the Metaphysical's recognition that the originality of what lies beyond the obvious may need an oblique presentation if it is to be properly expressed. Yet, in these days, he will also have to recognize that too many risks cannot be taken with the truth. Honesty of content is in shorter supply than cleverness of presentation. In a day of large-scale communication, the rule must be established that the larger the audience he addresses, the more scrupulous does the communicator have to be that he is speaking the truth, and the manifestly demonstrable truth. It is on this level above all others that the manufacture of 'pseudo-events' should be made most difficult and the distinction most sharply drawn between 'images' and the reality they are supposed to represent.

To place such emphasis on this in dealing with the British ideal may appear excessive, but it goes very near the root of a great deal of trouble. In a time when many of the old links of communal association have been weakened, the public scene becomes very much a matter of what is published, and publication, like everything else unless conscious efforts are made to resist the process, becomes increasingly centralized, standardized and trivialized.

New efforts have to be made today to purify the channels of communication. This is partly a matter for the media and their controllers but, just as politicians alone cannot be blamed for the lack of creative political ideas, so those who work in the media also depend on the way in which others do their job for their own effectiveness. Educational institutions and churches should be concerned above all else for honesty and truthfulness, self-criticism and mutual respect in communication, but, in their attempt to capture popular favour, they have sometimes been more influenced by the example of the media at their worst than determined to fulfill their proper function. This is one of the most obvious places where new standards need to be set in British public life.

The other place where higher standards are most obviously needed is in relation to participation in public affairs. 'Participation' has become a fashionable word, but as those who clamour for more participation quickly discover, more is needed than the right and opportunity to participate. The will to do so and the recognition that it requires trouble, effort and a sense of responsibility are much more important. The great weakness of British life on this level is what it always has been, that the majority of the population still have the mentality either of retainers or of pensioners. Conservatives like to have retainers, Socialists pensioners. Neither do enough to encourage a spirit of independent responsibility, nor will they be able to do so while politics and social life are seen so much in economic terms. Education should do a great deal to develop such a spirit, but it has become only too clear today that, left to itself, it is better at training for criticism than for commitment, especially when those being educated have, for all practical purposes, the status only of pensioners.

Most people today are ready to agree that 'the poorest he that is in England hath a life to live as the richest he'. Even Stanley Baldwin used to quote these words. What has not been so clearly seen is that he also has a right and responsibility to take his share in the making and the implementation of decisions. One of the reasons why the Free Churches and the Church of Scotland were so successful in the last century in engendering real participation was that they took this as axiomatic. These churches were the institutions of the people, and their leaders had little hesitation about driving home to their members, even the humblest, that their membership could not be fully realized without the acceptance of onerous responsibilities. Their very dignity demanded their accountability. But we have all become soft and flabby over these matters, not so much under the influence of social hand-outs, as opponents of the so called 'welfare state' allege, as through materialism, which arises from poverty of the imagination, or from cynicism, the product of an imagination turned sour. Apart from anything else, the complacency of the privileged, who tend to see participation only in terms of preserving their own economic advantage and social prestige, is at least as great as that of the not so privileged, who limit their loyalties to their own organized group.

Only a loyalty which transcends these limitations can enable people to break out of this situation, which is at the root of many of our present troubles, including a large part of economic inflation. There are many signs that people are hungry for such a loyalty, but none of our present social and political leaders nor any of our traditional institutions seem able to evoke it, and fortunately most people are still rightly suspicious of anyone who tries to compel participation through the use of over-simplified slogans which violate legitimate personal freedom. This aspect of the British ideal is still clearly visible, although a situation of social breakdown could easily obscure it. New insight is only likely to come piecemeal to individuals and small groups trying their hardest to discover fresh truth. Those who are responsible for the institutions of society cannot of themselves produce such individuals and groups, who must be moved by their own internal compulsions, but they can help create an environment which encourages rather than hinders them. Those who belong to Christian churches know that, above all others, they claim to be such institutions. How far are they able today to provide such an environment?

NOTES

1. Come to that, America herself has to face these problems, with Southern and Western institutions losing their distinctive identity through being swamped by Northerners wanting to study far away from home and in a congenial climate.

2. The authors of the Memorandum of Dissent in the report of *The Royal Commission on the Constitution*, Vol. II, may fail to do justice to the distinctiveness of Scottish and Welsh identity, but they have done a service in emphasizing this fact.

3. Gerhard Lenski, *The Religious Factor*, Doubleday, New York 1961.

4. See Eliot's revealingly polemical pamphlet written against the South India Church Union Scheme, *Reunion by Destruction*, Council for the Defence of Church Principles 1943, in which he saw Anglicanism exclusively in terms of this strain in the English tradition. See also his little-known lecture 'The English Tradition', *Christendom*, December 1940.

5. The most recent attempt to trace this succession is that of Professor David Martin in his chapter 'Dissenters and Abstainers', *A Sociology of English Religion*, pp. 15ff., but it is also described, in clear interrelation with its correlative attitude, in Kitson Clark's *The English Inheritance*.

6. It is interesting that, in practice, the kind of role that the monarch has come to play in our society has been more like that traditionally assigned to a mother than that of a father. This may explain why the monarchs who have been most successful as consensus figures in our history, Elizabeth I and Elizabeth II and Victoria, not to say the outstandingly popular Elizabeth the Queen Mother while she was Queen Consort, have been women.

7. To say that the Puritans hated beauty and denied vitality is a canard propagated by their opponents. This is not to deny that there were iconoclasts and philistines abroad in the seventeenth century and that they have operated under the cover of Puritan ideals, whether religious or secular, in later times, but the Puritan ideal was essentially positive and life-affirming.

8. David Martin, *The Religious and the Secular*, p. 41.

9. The correlative notion of 'the lady' never became so widespread, partly perhaps because in a dynamic social situation it was even more difficult exactly to define a lady than it was a gentleman, so that it has not suffered so spectacular an eclipse.

10. The most conservative among the powerful groups among the English, 'the landed gentry', remain unimpressed by the importance of higher education. They would applaud the remark attributed to Princess Anne and allegedly deleted from her pre-marriage television interview, that 'going to university is a much overrated pastime' (*The Times*, 13 November 1973).

11. It was said of John Keble, the father of the Oxford Movement, who would have deplored the theatrical character of much later Anglo-Catholicism, 'Popularity he shunned. Even to exercise influence, at least consciously, he had no care.' And Isaac Williams, a fellow-Tractarian, caught from Keble a 'horror and hatred of anything that seemed like display or the desire for applause or of immediate effect'. See B. M. G. Reardon, *From Coleridge to Gore*, Longman 1971, pp. 123f.

12. *Conversations at Little Gidding. Dialogues by Members of the Family*. Edited, with introductions and notes, by A. M. Williams, Cambridge University Press 1970.

13. When Dr Edmund Leach announced in his Reith Lectures for 1967 that man must now take the place of God because his scientific knowledge over his own nature and environment give him such great power, he was not taken with much seriousness. British people may not be sure that God is in heaven, but they are certain that man is on earth and that, in trying to do new things, he is more likely to succeed if he 'plays the game' according to rules which have been slowly worked out by trial and error than if he suddenly starts to 'play God'.

14. It was a significant act of solidarity on the part of Prince Charles when, after his investiture in 1970, he visited a *Gymanfa Ganu*, a Welsh hymn-singing festival, at Tabernacle Chapel, Morriston. In contrast to what happened in the investiture, here he was meeting a representative section of the Welsh community on their own terms on their home ground.

15. It was already possible to see this when my *Equality and Excellence*, SCM Press 1961, appeared, and the process has slowed down further, and on some levels gone into reverse, since that time.

16. Paul Johnson, *The Offshore Islanders*, Weidenfeld and Nicholson 1963, pp. 414–16.

17. Paul Johnson, op. cit., p. 417. And as Professor David Martin has remarked after considering some of the causes espoused by the intellectually self-conscious, 'Whatever the difficulties of institutional religion, they have little connection with any atrophy of the capacity for belief', *A Sociology of English Religion*, p. 76.

18. This is obviously true of Mr Johnson's book which, for all his enthusiasm for the philosophical radicals, is very much in the British tradition of a tract for the times written in the form of an essay in historical interpretation.

19. This is particularly true of the work of Dr J. H. Oldham and the many able people he influenced and inspired.

VI

JERUSALEM AND ALBION
The Christian Community and the Matter of Britain

'How can a man be born again when he is old?' Nicodemus' question was put to Jesus out of the experience of the old Israel, but the Christian community in modern Britain is in a good position to appreciate its sharpness and poignancy. The only direct answer is that such rebirth is impossible. As Nicodemus goes on to say, 'Can he enter his mother's womb again, and be born?' In other words, we are what we have become, and it is impossible to undo our history, going through the process of conception, birth, infancy and adolescence again, as though we had never reached maturity. Ours are old and tired churches, set within old and tired nations, and nothing can alter that fact.

Nothing can alter that fact, but Jesus' reply, indirect as it had to be, was not made to teach Nicodemus resignation but to enable him to see that nothing less costly and radical than rebirth was needed for renewal. Israel may stand in a special covenant-relation with God but, as far as her history and traditions are concerned, she has to operate under the same laws as any other human community. She grows old and is appointed to die. What is special about Israel is not her history and traditions as such but the insight given to her leaders in the very act of transmitting them that history and tradition, and the consciousness of distinctive identity they convey, are insufficient. As a teacher in Israel, Nicodemus should have known this, since it was part of his function to make Israel see that her life was to be found not in the Temple and the Law but in the call of God, who calls into question all earthly securities, including those which are the fruit of past faith, and demands venture into the unknown. This is why Jesus goes on to say that rebirth and entry into the kingdom are only possible through an understanding of what his crucifixion means for mankind.

This, the central message of the Christian faith, is reiterated week by week in sermon and sacrament, but every individual knows that it is the hardest thing in the world for him to come to terms with it in his own life. It is even harder for Christian institutions to do so, largely because, like the old Israel, they fail to see that it applies to them in their corporate capacity just as much as it does to individuals, and just as much as it does to other institutions. They think of it as a message they are commissioned to deliver to others rather than as one addressed in the first place to themselves, which they have to accept before what they say carries much conviction. The story of Nicodemus is a powerful reminder that this failure is to be expected and that there is rarely much point in berating churches for being old and tired, as prophetic spirits in their midsts are always eager to do, especially when they themselves are briefly sustained by the vitality and sharpened vision of natural youth. Evidence of decline can only be too easily detected in churches, as in other long-established institutions, and the decline usually takes easily predictable forms. What is much more interesting is whether any shoots of new life can be found struggling to emerge among their old stones.

Interesting as it may be, it is not a question which will be properly answered unless those who ask it realize how difficult new life is to detect and how qualified any answer has to be. This is particularly true at present, when people's conceptions of what constitutes vitality are both excessively romanticized and also strongly influenced by the values of the market-place, with their emphasis on eye-appeal and quick turnover. But gestation takes a long time and birth is a painful, messy and private process, and new life needs a great deal of nourishment and protection before it is able to stand on its own feet. Part of what the third chapter of the Gospel of John means by saying that new birth is possible only through being drawn to the cross of Christ is that the Christian life is a matter of effort, struggle and frequent failure, with the experience of renewal coming usually as a surprise, as grace which comes from beyond oneself at the limit of one's own endeavour.

How do the churches of Britain look today in the light of considerations such as these? Perhaps only one thing can be said about them with confidence, that they *are* old and tired and need renewal. This is not as depressing as it sounds because the realistic acceptance of one's situation is the first condition of being able to alter it. A great deal of Christian strategy in modern Britain, as in many other parts of the world, has been misdirected and therefore ineffective because it has not been based on this. It has concentrated on trying to induce institutional revival when the conditions of such revival have not been present, with the result that all that has been achieved has been the rhetoric of revival. This has devalued the spiritual currency and, over several generations, has made communication on a level where anything genuinely creative might happen increasingly difficult. It is of no use for institutions, any more than it is for individuals, to pretend that they are young and fresh and original when they are old and familiar and stale. Such actions only make them lose dignity and appear ridiculous. Christians who understand the faith they profess should be very good at doing what is required of them in a situation of this kind. They should act their age, accepting the fact that actions which might have been possible in the first flush of institutional youth are ruled out but that they can make the most of the not inconsiderable advantages of maturity and experience. Having seen a good deal of life, they should know how difficult new birth is, how it nearly always means a painful breach with the old and that the transition from the old to the new has to be handled with sensitivity and discrimination if unnecessary damage is to be avoided.

The implications of that general statement for the present situation of the British churches could not be more practical. They have to recognize that, in this situation, they are not likely to be very good at experiment and at breaking new ground and that they have to proceed cautiously. It is essential not to be misunderstood here. Rebirth is impossible without experiment and the breaking of new ground. Churches are very conservative institutions and, like others, are always glad to find excuses for maintaining familiar routines and avoiding the dislocation and difficulty of doing anything new. Nothing that is said here is meant to provide further material for such excuses, because, even in their present state, churches are perfectly capable of devoting much more of their time and energy than most of them do to what in other fields is called research and experiment. Their record is pitifully bad in this respect, even as compared with British business firms who, in their turn, compare very unfavourably with their American counterparts. What is essential is that churches should realize how hard and costly they are likely to find any worth-while attempt to do anything new in their present aged and tired state, and that if they are to be effective, they have to husband their resources very carefully to make the effort.

Things are better than they were, but the British churches have still not fully recovered from the aftermath of their phenomenal Victorian prosperity. The enormous popular success they achieved at that time went to the heads of many of them and they are only slowly waking up to greater sobriety.[1] The assumption still dies hard in conventional church circles that Christian communication should be easy and that, provided enough energy, self-confidence and skilful publicity are available, popularity and large crowds will return. As recently as the immediate post-war period, the Methodist church ran an evangelical campaign in London which they unblushingly described as a 'Christian Commando' campaign, and attempts are still made from time to time, although increasingly half-heartedly, to persuade hard-pressed churches to spend the considerable sums of money necessary for mounting advertising campaigns to 'promote' the Christian faith. It is true that recent experience in London theatres and in the cinema has shown that it is indeed possible to make a 'pop' impact with the Christian story, but what has not been proved is whether its impact is different from that of any other story offered in such a context. That is, the price of such popular success is that the impression left is shallow and transitory. Churches at their time of life can no longer afford to leave such impressions with people. They have purveyed cheap grace for so long that they have lost the habit of paying the necessary price of quality. In their efforts to ingratiate themselves with the public, too many have kept saying, like the man in the play, 'Never mind the quality, feel the width'. Before they can communicate again in such a way that anything creative occurs as a result of the encounter, the cost has to be counted. To achieve a new break-through in most branches of art in these days involves great effort and struggle and the acceptance of a very high failure rate. If anything, this is even more true in the dimension of religious experience, where many of the traditional channels of communication have become more worn and clogged with alien matter than they have in the arts and where the critical faculty has become much more highly developed than the appreciative. People are not willing to 'attend', in Simone Weil's sense, and it is only when they give that kind of concentration that they are able to perceive the truth of which Christian faith speaks. The first consequence, therefore, of their recognition of how old and tired they are on the part of churches is an acceptance of the difficulty of experiment and of the need for patience and realism in appraising its results.

A second implication is that they are likely to be better at conservation than at breaking new ground. Here again it is necessary to safeguard ourselves against misunderstanding and to strike a right balance. Churches in Britain receive every encouragement to fulfil a conservationist function. Quite apart from their own inherent conservatism, they are most commonly thought of by others as repositories of our Christian and national past. They remain the most suitable places that the vast majority of people can think of to receive our lifeless bodies when they are gathered to their fathers, but they are rarely thought of as centres of new vitality and of hope for the future in this world. I once asked a well-known academic student of popular culture whether he would address a meeting on how he saw the cultural role of churches in modern Britain, emphasizing that he could be as critical as he liked. He declined, saying that he was not accustomed to thinking of churches in this way, which was, perhaps, itself significant.

Whether he was right or wrong in having such an attitude, it is undoubtedly one which would be shared by many.

So much is this the case that most churchmen concerned for renewal prefer not to discuss their conservationist role, lest it might divert energies which can be ill-spared from the more urgent tasks of making experiments and promoting change. That is understandable, but there is no evading the fact that all churches have to do an enormous amount of conservation. If we try to ignore it, all that will happen is that the work of conservation will be done with a wrong set of priorities, sentimentally and defensively and taking the line of least resistance, instead of with the discrimination and imagination which are necessary. Churches may be equipped to be better at conservation than at experiment. This does not mean that conservation will be easy or that to bring a Christian judgment to bear upon it will not involve showing courage and originality.

This is a point which churchmen should be able to grasp more readily than the servants of many other institutions, because a great deal of distinctive Christian intellectual activity is directed to helping them to see it. The Christian community lives by memory and hope. It stands in a special relation to the past because it is events in the past, and the interpretation vindicated by later events which arose out of them, which determines the community's shape in the present and provides it with pointers for the future. This is why, in worship and in thought, it is always recalling itself to its origins, not out of nostalgia or ancestral piety, but strictly in order to rediscover the right frame of reference in which to act here and now. For the churches' origins are of special character, lying in events which uncover the permanent elements in the human situation before God, in which all people share. These are always being obscured by the exigencies of the passing moment which lead everyone, including members of churches, to do anything except wait upon God. It is only when this kind of reference to the past is made that anything which could begin to be claimed as God's guidance for the future can be discerned. The testimony of those who speak of Christ out of the past is that he made himself known to them as the possessor of the key to the future, and it is when the Christian community makes the effort to stand alongside him as he is known out of the past that it can have any confidence that it is his future which it is helping to form. Otherwise, it does no more than carry on like any other institutions concerned for its own secular well-being, trying to strengthen itself within established patterns. When in the present they have this kind of perspective on what they have inherited as human institutions among others from their past, churches can find the necessary detachment and independence which will enable them to decide what to preserve and what to discard in faithfulness to their own vocation.

This matters a great deal in these days just because the conservationist role of churches is becoming more widely appreciated. One of the signs of this is the remarkable ease with which cathedrals and other large churches are able to raise money for their repair and maintenance.[2] No other institutions, except for a few highly privileged Oxbridge colleges, could raise private money so readily. The roots of these Christian institutions lie very deep in British soil. Earnest Christians, and many others, may believe that they need more drastic pruning and more grafting than sentimental admirers might welcome and timid gardeners provide, but very few people want to uproot them and anyone who tried, from whatever motives, would quickly discover what a formidable task it was. Harassed ecclesiastical administrators, struggling to achieve redeployment, have long since realized that the only operation more difficult than that of filling a church in modern Britain is that of closing one.[3]

With the growth of a greater understanding of what is involved in the process of conservation, this state of affairs is likely to become more and not less true in the near future. Genuine conservation is being seen as a matter of much more than merely preserving the shells of beautiful buildings, abstracted from their traditional function and setting. The mistakes of policies of ruthless 'comprehensive redevelopment' have made it clear that conservation has to pay attention to continuity of use, spirit and style as well as physical preservation. Thus, to turn redundant churches into museums or branch libraries or scout headquarters may often be inevitable and sensible, but usually it is only a second-best form of conservation. Churches can welcome this more sympathetic attitude, yet from their point of view it obviously still has its dangers. When conservation becomes the vogue, it is tempting to accept purely antiquarian or aesthetic criteria of judgment rather than distinctively Christian ones. Antiquarian and aesthetic considerations must carry weight with Christians, but they should rarely be decisive.

The theme of this book has been the way in which religious heritage and national consciousness are bound up with each other in the life of Britain, and it has tried to redefine their relation to each other in a Christian context. Yet the importance of this theme in no way detracts from the no less important truth that the chief reason why British churches are weak today is that they do not believe enough in the Christian God whom they profess to serve. This is why they lack the vitality and the independence of judgment to stand back from their own situation and see themselves and their relation to the society of which they are part in the right perspective and then to speak with prophetic authority.

This decline of distinctive Christian conviction on the part of churches themselves has one aspect which is particularly closely related to our present theme. We have seen that the main strength of the British ideal has lain in its ability to hold together in tension the two chief strains in our history at their best and that much of our recent weakness has been due to the relaxation of this tension. This has led to intellectual complacency and sloth. The British churches have to confess that they possess their full share of these. This is not to say that, as some of their sterner critics allege, they have become intellectually bankrupt. A juster, and perhaps even more damaging charge, would be that they have not shown enough intellectual enterprise to run the risk of bankruptcy, contenting themselves with small, apparently safe, investments and very modest returns, with the consequent result that over the years they have suffered a fate not unlike that of the holders of Government Bonds.

Theological renewal depends ultimately on spiritual renewal, and this cannot be induced by any means within ordinary human control. Why conviction concerning theological truth can be relatively clear and luminous in one age and clouded in another is a mystery. But Christians should have enough experience of the ups and downs of the life of the spirit to know how to behave responsibly in times when there is little 'open vision'. They can, at least, attend with special care and humility to the best insights of the Christian past and strive to be as alert and intellectually disciplined in their own situation as possible, refusing to be tossed to and fro by passing fashion as they do so. It would be hard to claim that typical Christian proclamation in Britain over the last couple of generations has displayed these qualities very clearly.

The small-scale Christian revival of the 1940s and early 1950s did find some theological expression, yet it never succeeded in reaching more than a small public, and as the 1950s moved into the 1960s, its impetus seemed to be lost. The extraordinary public interest aroused by Bishop Robinson's *Honest to God*, in itself a modest enough essay in theological restatement, suggests the presence of a deep, unsatisfied hunger for theological illumination. For some reason, many ministers and clergy refuse to believe this. The grounds for this conviction would be clearer if they themselves had made more strenuous efforts to offer such illumination and had been rejected.[4] Their reluctance to make them may owe as much to the confusion and lethargy they share with the rest of society as to any inherent difficulty in the undertaking. When serious people outside the churches begin to hear those inside arguing passionately with each other about theological matters, not out of contentiousness or a desire to impress outsiders but from a conviction that the answers to their questions make a significant difference to the way they themselves live, they will prick up their ears. Some of them may even be moved to learn the terms of the argument, so that they can have part in it. What is missing in many church people today is precisely this strong conviction of the importance of their own distinctive activity, especially on the intellectual side, which drives them to undertake it regardless of whether others choose to be interested or not.

This is, of course, not for a moment to imply that church people should now become self-preoccupied and indifferent to the world around them. It is simply to say again, as the early leaders of the ecumenical movement like Dr Visser 't Hooft saw so clearly, that theological revival is the necessary condition of revived cultural awareness and effective social criticism. Without it, as we are already seeing in Britain and elsewhere, the revival of national self-consciousness only arouses the resentful self-righteousness which misuses theology as the tool of nationalist ideology. It is only when churches regain the authority which belongs to the distinctive contribution that they have to make to communal life that they will have the right to be heard on their own terms. They are very reluctant to acknowledge that this will be impossible without more hard, disciplined, practical theological work than most of them have undertaken in modern Britain.

They are a long way from regaining the authority inherent in their proper function but perhaps they can begin to put themselves on the way towards it by, at least, recapturing enough self-confidence about that distinctive contribution to fulfil the educational responsibilities within society to which they are already committed and to reopen conversation with representatives of other institutions in society. The church's primary mission is evangelization, but one of the facts old and tired churches have to face about themselves is that they are not likely to be good at direct attempts at evangelization. Charismatic individuals sustained by strong conviction may be able to unstop the deaf ears, and when that happens it will provide its own justification, but the institution itself is unlikely to be able to. When it tries, what usually happens is that the good news sounds like stale news. This is, of course, widely recognized. 'Dialogue' has been a favourite word of Christian apologists for the last generation and 'education' is what most professional Christian workers have been trying to do for most of their time. Yet the conversation and the education have not always been conducted with the assurance which derives from belief in the truth of one's own distinctive position. Christian spokesmen give the impression that they are on the defensive against opponents who hold stronger weapons in their hands. Formal Christian education, in particular, has suffered recently from a chronic sense of insecurity about its own status as a subject. This may be partly due to its singularly unfortunate position in many parts of the state system, that of being protected without having adequate resources and scope for genuine influence, for all the world as though it were too infantile to stand on its own two feet. Perhaps the chief reason why the majority of English people in particular treat religion so amiably but with such a lack of serious interest is that, as Professor David Martin has observed, 'the central figure for teaching Christianity is a lady in a primary school'.[5] Those who take over the task of Christian religious education from that admirable lady may be able to give greater stability and imaginative power to their subject if they present it as an indispensable introduction to self-understanding through showing how classic Christian faith constantly interacts with British history, literature and culture.

The same attitude should be displayed in wider fields than those of formal education. The difficulties of Christian communication today are notorious. Christian spokesmen, and especially professional Christian spokesmen, know how easy it is to say the wrong thing or to say the right thing in the wrong way. Those who lack Christian belief or are confused about the matter are often defensive when they are not arrogant and are quick to take umbrage and break off from conversation. Fortunately, few of the more thoughtful among them have a similar attitude to those parts of the Christian past which are available for present enjoyment. This is true whether it be in art or architecture or music or poetry or ancient custom or even in theology itself when it wears a comely enough literary dress. It is here that the Christian spokesman should reveal his skill in discriminating conservation, by helping to present these treasures in such a way that they speak for themselves and raise their own questions for life today in the minds of those who appreciate them, with the minimum of intrusion by his irritating self.

This goes against the grain for professional churchmen because they have long been accustomed to suppose that their duty is to force the issue upon reluctant hearers and then to exhort and to inspire. Today, they must face the fact that efforts to force the issue, exhort and inspire, often fall upon deaf ears and that the deafness is caused in part by themselves and the old and tired institutions which they represent. Their attitude, therefore, has to combine confidence in the power of Christian truth to commend itself to others once it is really heard with humility about their own ability to make others hear it.

This humility about themselves and about the present state of churches need not express itself in disparagement of the Christian heritage of Britain and of the separate nations which make it up. On the contrary, the present situation calls for a strong reassertion of its value. To be free of pretensions about themselves also releases Christians from any need to be impressed by the pretensions of their contemporaries, especially those of them who give themselves the airs of great enlightenment as 'secular' men. Whatever they may choose to call themselves, they live in and have been formed by a community which has been deeply coloured throughout its history by the Christian faith and they cannot understand themselves unless they recognize this. What is important is that Christian spokesmen should point this out, not in a scolding or querulous way but with an appropriate sense of privilege that they are themselves able to acknowledge, cherish and interpret that Christian heritage, and perhaps in a small way extend it. This will enable them to recapture the attitude of patient and relaxed assurance which a good teacher has, one who is confident without being either defensive or patronizing, because he knows that the subject-matter is able to impose its own authority upon others as it has upon himself.

This attitude is needed if difficulties which arise within churches themselves in these days are to be properly handled. In his study of *The Social Significance of Church Membership in the Borough of Falkirk* which has been quoted earlier, Peter Sissons makes a distinction between what he calls communal and associational Christians, between those who take their church membership for granted, as of a piece with their membership of the wider community, as part of what it means to be Scots and to live in Falkirk, and those whose church membership is a matter of reflection and deliberate commitment as over against alternative possibilities. Anyone closely familiar with church life, especially in old-established neighbourhoods, will know how real this distinction is and how much friction it generates.[6] The associationalists accuse the communalists of being mere culture-Christians, more concerned with the well-being of their own congregation or denomination as an institution reflecting the traditional values of their own neighbourhood or segment of the nation than with furthering the cause of the universal Christ. The communalists, in their turn, dismiss the associationalists as rootless enthusiasts, who love to espouse liberal or 'progressive' causes but who have no depth and no staying power, often living in that neighbourhood only for a short time and more interested in discussion and general ideas than in unspectacular activity in the enduring local situation. These two groups, who are to be found in these days in all churches, reflect, in however diluted a form, the classical conservative-radical tension of British life, and the detachment which comes from an appreciation of the value of that tension can help make their relation constructive. The extent to which communalists have drifted away from churches in recent years, although more in England and Wales than in Scotland, shows how essential are the fresh conviction and new insight on which the associationalists lay such stress if the churches are to flourish. Yet the fact remains that most people are communalist rather than associationalist in temperament and outlook, and they are only able to participate in renewal when it is related in ways they can grasp to their own community and its history and traditions. Renewal is possible only through the activity of associationalists, but it will be ineffective until it begins to express itself through the existing patterns of social relationships. The only alternative is social revolution, which creates such immense problems that British people have always rejected it as self-defeating. A revival of communal loyalty without fresh vision will be a mere conservative reaction. On the other hand, a rebirth of Christian conviction, and of the ecumenical zeal which in these days must go with it, which is cut off from the deep springs of communal loyalty, will find that all it does is to substitute dramatic gestures for significant actions.

This attitude should also govern the approach of churches to the other major task which confronts them along with conservation, that of reorganization and redeployment. These are imperative for churches which have become old and tired, yet they are the most delicate and tricky of operations for institutions at this stage of their development, especially institutions with such deep roots and such subtle interconnections with the rest of society. The impatience of the religious cosmopolitan and the short-sightedness of the localist can be equally damaging in this situation, yet the insight of the one and the experience and loyalty of the other are equally essential.

To give an example, reforming churchmen, especially in the Church of England, often argue that the traditional British parochial systems have had their day, because they presuppose the existence of a static Christendom which has long since vanished. The truth of this for large cities and towns has long been obvious and the pressure of circumstances has led to substantial modifications but, they would argue, the process has not gone anything like far enough. A new pattern of church organization is slowly emerging in Britain, that which expresses itself in what might be called the cathedral, the chaplaincy and the conventicle.[7] The modern Christian community needs large centres where its members can gather to express their concern for life in its unity as well as in its variety. The great Anglican cathedrals are best placed to meet this need and it is significant that, almost in despite of themselves in some instances, they have taken on a new lease of life as centres of communal celebration and reflection. The new Coventry Cathedral is the most striking example, but anyone who studies the programmes of many British cathedrals today and sees the vast crowds pouring into them, not all of them simply as tourists, must wonder whether there is not here a great communal need which is still only imperfectly met. The Christian community also needs to exist within the major institutions of society with their specialized patterns of life, and to exist in a way which is governed by those patterns rather than by the church's own developed form. This we call the chaplaincy. Dr Paul estimates that a quarter of the ordained ministry of the Church of England will need to be engaged in servicing activities of this kind in a variety of institutions before very long. And finally, the small church, of the familiar suburban type which still flourishes, close to people's homes and organized around the family and its leisure-time activities, will continue to be indispensable. It is worth describing it by the slight derogatory title of the conventicle not simply for the sake of alliteration but to underline its incomplete nature, because many people still take it to be the normative form of church life when it is no more than one vital part. This may be made clearer as family-based churches increasingly break down into even smaller units, such as house groups.

Church reform needs to press forward along these lines, but a great deal of frustration can be avoided, and the alienation of many 'communalists' prevented, if at the same time it is recognized that, in many parts of Britain, older patterns of church organization are still likely to function better than new ones and that it is desirable to leave well alone. The parochial system, for example, is still a reality in many of the small towns and some parts of the country-side in England and Scotland. Even when it has to be modified, it is wise to show respect for it in stable neighbourhoods where it is linked to many other communal forms of association in ways which no longer exist in most neighbourhoods of large cities. And as we have emphasized throughout, it is essential to show respect for the way in which religious commitment and the sense of national identity are intertwined. Apart from anything else this helps to maintain that balance between conservatism and change to which British life has always aspired. It is true that churches are much less vulnerable to the temptations of 'comprehensive redevelopment' than most other bodies, but they also are not immune from the influence of fashionable slogans.

What, on the basis of present probabilities, is likely to be the way in which relations between churches in Britain are going to develop over the next generation? Once the present disappointment is overcome, the Church of England will finally manage to unite, or at least, achieve much closer relationship with the Methodists, and after that, the union of the new Church of England with the new United Reformed Church will seem to be the obvious next move. In this situation, the Church of England will be overwhelmingly the dominant partner. Past experience does nothing to suggest that the terms for such a merger will be generous, and we should then be left with a situation in England where old mainline Dissent, along with the great Methodist tradition, will virtually have ceased to exist. It is true that the Baptists will probably continue to stand apart but, in their isolation, their evangelical wing, already relatively stronger than their liberal wing in these days, will be predominant, forming links with other evangelical groups to make a new kind of dissenting churchmanship, but one which, initially at least, would have little interest in public affairs and the 'matter of Britain'. The Quakers will remain as an option for some, but on a small scale. The Welsh will concentrate on themselves, making it a matter of pride to be indifferent to what is happening in England, and salving their ecumenical consciences by trying to achieve the union of Welsh-speaking denominations on the basis of a renewed sense of Welsh identity, a union which would probably be achieved only between the Calvinistic and Wesleyan Methodists and the Independents. What will happen to Rome is hardest of all to forecast, and this may well prove to be the factor which will throw all calculations into confusion, but if something like the present leadership in Westminster continues, the probability is that, while the improvement in relations will be maintained, no radical institutional changes will be allowed to take place in this generation. Meanwhile, the Church of Scotland will remain not very interested in anything outside Scotland in Britain except for talking with the national church of the English and will maintain the search for a *modus vivendi* with the Church of England which does not impair its independence nor wound its pride. Whether it will succeed will depend on the negotiating skill of the enlarged Church of England and on the degree of persistence of Scottish suspicion of anything English, especially in ecclesiastical guise.

If things were to work out in this way, and of course any such prognostication must be tentative in the extreme, would it give any grounds for dissatisfaction? Most church people would probably think not. After all, reunion is a good thing. The remnants of the social harm done by ecclesiastical division in the past still exist, and it is time they were disposed of. The adjustments involved in moving in together would have a stimulating effect on old and tired churches and might give them at least a measure of new life. The redeployment of resources which is so necessary and which has still a long way to go would be made incomparably easier.

True as this may be as far as it goes, reunion in Britain along the lines we have envisaged would create an unsatisfactory situation. It would, in fact, represent an Anglican victory and with it a victory for the Anglican view of English and British life. The vital tension between differing attitudes which has been the chief source of our social health would cease and church and society would sink even deeper into a featureless mediocrity. It is essential for the well-being of the *church* as a Christian community that there should be a more thorough confrontation between the distinctively Anglican theological attitude, with as much attention paid to its special interpretation of the nature of the incarnation and its notion of universal law as justifying its organic view of society and institutional continuity as to its unique doctrine of 'the historic episcopate', and the attitude of the more fully Reformed churches, with their greater emphasis on the transcendent sovereignty of God and his freedom in relation to the church. The theological debate has to take place within a different context from that of the 1930s and the 1940s, and some of the issues which exercised us greatly then, such as those to do with the doctrine of the ministry and inter-communion, may need much less attention, but unresolved issues remain. They will not go away, even if, in a well-intentioned desire to have some kind of institutional reunion to show for ourselves by 1980, church leaders prefer to ignore them. Likewise, it is no less essential for the well-being of British *society* that the only remotely viable conception of an 'alternative society' which these islands have ever produced, that of the more radical form of Protestantism which found most of its political expression through the Liberal Party and the Labour movement, should continue to be represented adequately in the conversation of the churches about British life. This is not because those who cherish this conception have a monopoly of social virtue. On the contrary, as we have already seen from our consideration of the English Free Churches and Scotland and Wales, their limitations have been clearly enough exposed in the course of our history. Yet the fact remains that the tension engendered by their relation with the dominant English and Anglican attitude has been essential to our social health and any genuinely creative reunion must maintain it or replace it with something better, and not simply relax it.

The role of the Church of Scotland in this situation could be crucial. She is far better equipped than any other church in Britain to ensure that the discussion concerning reunion could be both theologically and socially adequate, but to do so requires a change of attitude on her part. She must stop thinking of herself as, above all else, the church of the Scottish nation, which she only partially represents, and see herself much more as a church of the Reformed family, with close and extensive international links. This should not be impossible because it is congruous with her best traditions, those of Knox and the Confession of 1560 rather than those of the self-righteous Solemn League and Covenant. The English Free Churches are too weak and those of Wales too preoccupied with themselves to be effective in representing the Reformed cause in British life without the informed and committed leadership of the Church of Scotland. And in conversations with Roman Catholicism, which are likely to be increasingly important, the Church of Scotland may have a more important part to play than at might first appear. Their theological differences may be sharper, but many Scots Presbyterians have more affinity with the rank and file of British Catholics, who are of Scots or Irish or continental European background and often working-class, than have most articulate Anglicans. They all share a minority status in British life which means that, on some levels at least, the Church of Scotland could act as a useful 'bridge-church' between Rome and Canterbury.

The Church of Scotland also has a neglected importance in the context of British church relations with the wider world. The Reformed communion is one of the major sections of the Christian community in the whole world. Reformed churches are strong in some Common Market countries and exceptionally strong in the USA, and they are displaying remarkable vitality in such rapidly developing countries as Brazil and Indonesia. What they have to say should affect our understanding of ourselves in this country. This need not be said in any spirit of revived Reformed confessionalism. No churches are more committed to ecumenism than the Reformed, who have produced many of the ecumenical movement's outstanding leaders, but ecumenism has always meant that particular churches and groups of churches should make their distinctive contributions. In the context of the Christian community as a whole, it is essential that reunion in Britain should not be seen too much in terms of the Anglican communion alone.

The founders of the modern ecumenical movement had a degree of insight which enabled them to see beyond the possibilities of their immediate situation and to lay far-reaching plans. They have largely been justified in the event. Similar insight is badly needed today. The gifts of far-sighted statesmanship no longer seem to be cultivated in the British Christian community. For all their weaknesses, the British churches are not so tired or despondent as to merit such lack of interest in their future. The Christian bond between the peoples of England, Scotland and Wales remains a strong one, and in a time when the political strains between them seem to be intensifying, the churches have a special responsibility to improve the quality of that bond, so that it can become a source of self-criticism and reconciliation rather than a cause of division. Otherwise, relations between the countries will become largely a matter of competition over economic benefits and Scottish and Welsh efforts to squeeze political concessions out of the reluctant English.

Churches can help to strengthen this bond if they take care to ensure that a wide enough range of people are consulted when they reach decisions about reorganization and redeployment. This is particularly important in relation to schemes for reunion, which are major occasions for precipitating reorganization. Naturally enough, those most involved in discussion of these matters, especially with reference to reunion, are the current holders of office in the church's national organizations. Their tendency is to think of reorganization first in terms of the adaptation of existing national structures to each other, with the minimum amount of institutional dislocation. Nothing is more understandable, but churches of all bodies should be alert to the dangers of such a procedure, which are that they will reinforce the already strong centralizing pressures of modern life and increase the power of officials at the centre. The short-term interests of local congregations or regions are likely to prompt people to resist this, but those representing these interests often have too narrow a view of all the factors to be taken into account, generally far narrower than that of the national officers, who are at least in a position to see how much change is needed. The people who are rarely consulted and who might have a great deal to contribute are those who are involved with the other institutions of society as they impinge on the churches, and with the British community and its heritage as a whole. Politicians, writers, sociologists, architects and those who might be able to interpret the views of normally inarticulate sections of the community, such as some social workers and trade union officers, are all people who might have ideas about the social role of churches and their future shape which the churches might well take into account. This could be true even when these people are not regular churchgoers. The invitation to think seriously about these matters, perhaps for the first time, will often prompt them to think afresh about their own relation to churches. It need hardly be said that this implies no devaluation of the discussion of distinctively theological insights nor even of the traditional ecclesiastical preoccupation with matters of liturgy and church order. What it does assert is that, on the level of institutional reorganization and of possible redeployment of resources, the interests of those primarily concerned with the adjustment of existing denominational structures to each other are by no means the only ones to be taken into account, and that it needs a conscious change of policy to prevent their interests being all-determinative. This is one way of helping reunited churches to ensure that the dialectic between conservatism and radicalism which is essential to social health is retained in their own life.

The Christian redeployment demanded today, however, carries wider implications than those which deal only with the future shape of churches as institutions. As the way of life of large sections of the British community becomes increasingly divorced from Christian standards, the temptation grows for Christians to make their faith only a matter of private conviction and to cease to be interested in the quality of the other institutions of society, or, if they are involved in them, to assume that a Christian judgment cannot be brought to bear upon them since so many who belong to them do not acknowledge Christian faith. This is the way taken by many conservative evangelicals, whose numbers are growing significantly in these days. But this is to overlook that Christians have always lived in a mixed society and that Christian moral guidance is not given for ideal situations but for the confused world which actually exists. More than that, a great deal of evidence is available, notably in the still relevant although now neglected work of Reinhold Niebuhr, about how to conduct ourselves in such a society. If professional churchmen do well to consult experts in other fields about the future shape of the churches, they should also see more clearly how much they can help the other institutions of society fulfil their own functions more effectively, without in any way impinging on their proper autonomy. This, after all, is what is meant to lie behind the reorganization of church life in terms of cathedrals, chaplaincies and conventicles, which is already beginning to take shape before our eyes. There is a great deal of talk in church circles today of the church as a 'servant church', but much of it is still in terms of participation by church people, and often enough the church's own professional servants, in 'communicare' activities. That may be useful as far as it goes, but something both wider in scope and more distinctive is needed. The worlds of politics, law, industry, commerce, defence and education all need 'the servant church', not in order to tell them what to do from the outside but to help those within these worlds to do their duty more effectively. This is why the work of 'chaplaincy', in which the role of clerical professionals is strictly subordinate to that of committed lay people who have responsibilities in these fields, is particularly important, although it demands for its fulfilment the 'cathedral's' emphasis on society as a whole and the 'conventicle's' awareness of what life is like in the home and its immediate neighbourhood. While internal revival is the condition of ecclesiastical redeployment, it will not be effective without expressing itself in a fresh concern for the internal renewal of the other institutions of British society.

If churches are to redeploy from strength and not from weakness, it is essential that they should make the most of the opportunities which are presented to them by the reduction of their institutional strength. Ecclesiastical buffer-states between God's kingdom and the world are always growing up and extending their empires. The particularly extensive and extravagant one which grew up in Victorian times still lingers on and its remnants still need to be swept away, especially those which encourage unrealistic expectations about the size of the paid staffs greatly diminished churches can recruit and maintain. To change the metaphor, in the slimming operation that the church has to undergo today, she still has a good deal of fat and flabbiness to get rid of before she can undertake the vigorous, quick-footed action her situation requires and before the beauty of her true shape is again visible to the world.

The parable of the prodigal son throws a searching light not only on what is called the secularizing process in the modern world but also on what the reaction of churchmen towards it should be. After a period when the household has known prosperity, younger sons, who might be taken to represent those who do not feel called to have the chief responsibility for carrying on the family and its home, seem to find it irresistible to claim their part of the inheritance and go off into the far country, seeking their own fortune unhindered by domestic restraints. While they are still living on the richness and strength which comes from their inheritance, their 'emancipated' life in the far country seems initially to be far more exciting than anything they knew at home. But as more and more of what they have received is used up, whether in riotous living or in less spectacular ways, the difficulty of its replacement with anything new is revealed, and the poverty of life cut off from its source becomes increasingly hard to bear.

Those who know the love and power of the Father can be confident that, in due time, the prodigals will come to themselves and want to return. It will be at this point that they will do well to remember that the parable was addressed to the older, not the younger, brother. It is not for those who have remained at home in our society either to show the censoriousness of the older brother or, what may be an even greater danger in these days, officiously to arrogate to themselves the initiative of the Father. Their task is to make it easy for the younger brothers, once their Father has made his peace with them, to take their place again in the household, remembering in doing so that family relationships are always complicated, even in reconciliation. If any expression of private gratification is to be allowed to them, let it only be that of quiet pleasure at the surprise of the returned prodigals in discovering how much of the family heritage has been maintained in their absence and how many improvements have been made in the old home.

NOTES

1. Professor Owen Chadwick points out that, although the proportion of the population in the churches declined in Victoria's reign, the actual numbers, especially in towns, grew spectacularly because of the rapid growth of the population as a whole. As institutions they had a psychology, and often an ideology, of success. See Owen Chadwick, 'The Established Church under Attack', in Anthony Symondson (ed.), *The Victorian Crisis of Faith*, SPCK 1970, pp. 94f.

2. Some striking statistics are provided by Trevor Beeson, *The Church of England in Crisis*, Davis-Poynter 1973, p. 141.

3. The problems they can run into are vividly described by Leslie Paul, *A Church by Daylight*, Geoffrey Chapman 1973, p. 150.

4. Even in 1950, when the situation was so much better than it is today, Dr Kitson Clark was constrained to observe, on the very last page of his discussion of the English heritage, 'Christians must not only, as they are often told, be worthy of their faith but, as they are not so often told, they must understand it and be ready to explain it', op. cit., p. 181.

5. David Martin, *A Sociology of English Religion*, pp. 88f.

6. David B. Clarke, 'Local and Cosmopolitan Aspects of Religious Activity in a Northern Suburb: Process of Change', *Sociological Yearbook of Religion in Britain* 4, SCM Press 1971, pp. 141-59, gives an account of these in his study of church members in a neighbourhood in the North of England, where he makes a similar, if not exactly identical, distinction between 'localists' and 'cosmopolitans'.

7. The most systematic observer of modern Anglican church life, Dr Leslie Paul, sees a threefold pattern of this kind emerging in the Church of England, though he gives the elements slightly different names. See Leslie Paul, *A Church by Daylight*, Part V, chs. 8-10.

Index